# Exploring Languages

# Languages

## A Complete Introduction for Foreign Language Students

**Dora Kennedy**

**Pat Barr-Harrison**
**Maria Guarrera Wilmeth**

 National Textbook Company
a division of *NTC Publishing Group* • Lincolnwood, Illinois USA

The contributions of Clarence Wachner
are gratefully acknowledged.

Published by National Textbook Company, a division of NTC Publishing Group.
© 1994 by NTC Publishing Group, 4255 West Touhy Avenue,
Lincolnwood, (Chicago), Illinois 60646-1975 U.S.A.
Manufactured in the United States of America.

4 5 6 7 8 9 0 VP 9 8 7 6 5 4 3 2 1

# EXPLORING LANGUAGES

## CONTENTS

Message to Students                                                v

## Part 1: Exploring the World of Languages

Chapter 1    Communicating for World Understanding              2
Chapter 2    Signs and Symbols, including Esperanto             9
Chapter 3    Your Language and Mine and How It Came to Be      22
Chapter 4    Families of Languages: Their Similarities and
             Differences                                       41

## Part 2: Exploring Languages of the World

Chapter 5    Exploring Spanish and the Hispanic World          50
Chapter 6    Exploring French and the French-Speaking World    74
Chapter 7    Exploring German and German-Speaking Areas        93
Chapter 8    Exploring Italian, Italy, and Its People         109
Chapter 9    Exploring Russian, Russia, and Its People        126
Chapter 10   Exploring Japanese, Japan, and Its People        143
Chapter 11   Exploring Chinese, China, and Its People         158
Chapter 12   Exploring Arabic and the Arabic-Speaking World   171
Chapter 13   Exploring the Hebrew Language, Israel,
             and Its People                                   185
Chapter 14   Exploring Swahili and Swahili-Speaking Areas     196
Chapter 15   Exploring Latin, Ancient Rome, and Its People    210
Chapter 16   Exploring Ancient Greek and the
             Ancient Greek World                              227

Our planet is home to many peoples, cultures, and languages.

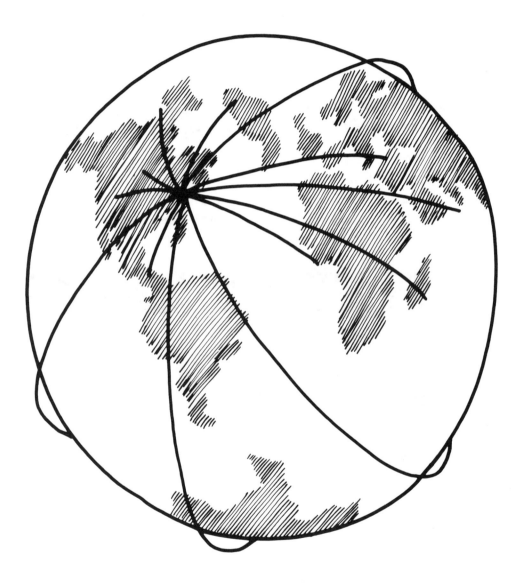

To see the earth as it truly is, small and blue and beautiful in that eternal silence where it floats, is to see ourselves as riders on the earth together... —Archibald MacLeish

# Message to the Students

This book introduces you to some of the world's most important languages.

Do you know how many languages are spoken on earth? More than three thousand! We are going to explore those that are most widely used, including English.

Have you ever thought about why we should study foreign languages? One important reason is that our country needs citizens who can communicate with people of other lands. You can become a better communicator by learning even a little of another language. In addition to helping visitors who come to our country, you may have opportunities in your future career to use your knowledge of a foreign language.

Have you ever wondered: What is language? You will learn more about the answer to this question as you do the activities and projects in this book. You will find out some things about how language developed, how English is related to other languages, and how some languages have been invented for specific purposes.

We hope the experience of exploring many languages will not only help you decide to study a foreign language, but will also increase your word power in English as well.

# PART ONE

# Exploring
# the World
# of Languages

# COMMUNICATING
## FOR WORLD
## UNDERSTANDING

## How We Communicate

### The First Exchange of Ideas

Nobody knows how old human speech is. Many believe that signs and gestures were the first form of language. Some of the gestures were probably accompanied by sounds, such as grunts and growls.

Human language involves communication and exchange of ideas. Scientists have also been investigating language in animals such as apes and dolphins. You may want to investigate this topic of animal communication.

# hello in...

| | |
|---|---|
| Spanish | ¡Hola! |
| Russian | Привет! |
| Latin | Salve! |
| German | Guten Tag! |
| French | Bonjour! |
| Italian | Ciao! |
| Japanese | こんにちは。 |

Consider ways that people communicate ideas. A basic way, of course, is with words. But what about gestures, signs, sounds, pictures, and music?

Each of the examples below represents a communication system. What does each communicate?

| | |
|---|---|
| boat whistle | siren |
| lighthouse | foghorn |
| barber pole | flag |
| flares | road sign |
| BASIC (computer language) | uniforms |
| fireworks | skull and crossbones |

Did you know that computers also need language? Special languages are designed for communicating with computers, so that they can be told what to do. Have you heard of BASIC? This is the language that is used with most home and school computers. If you have a computer, you may have learned how to write programs for it in BASIC. You may learn PASCAL and other computer languages later in your studies.

## Language Sounds Have Meaning

Humans have learned to produce many different sounds and to combine these sounds into words and sentences within different language systems.

English is only one of these language systems. Here is a problem for you. Suppose a new student has enrolled in your school. You meet her in the hall after class. She looks worried, and she says to you, "¿Dónde está el teléfono? Tengo que llamar a mi mamá." Would you know what she said? Could you help her?

You wouldn't know what she was asking if you hadn't heard those sounds before. Did you recognize any of the words? Maybe you recognized *teléfono* and *mamá*. Perhaps she used gestures to get her idea across to you.

As you help her find the telephone so she can call her mother, you realize what it means to *understand* another language when you hear it. First of all, you must understand the *sounds*. You must understand the words that the sounds make. In reading, you must recognize the *written symbols* that make up words.

By the way, do you know what language the new student was speaking? If you think it is Spanish, you are correct!

Spanish is just one of the world's languages. On just one continent—in Africa—more than eight hundred languages are spoken. These include Yoruba, Swahili, and even French. In Asia—Chinese, Korean, and Vietnamese are some of the languages spoken; in Europe—Italian, Dutch, and German. These are only a few examples. Find out the names of other languages and where they are spoken.

Children usually learn the language that is spoken in their home when they are small. They also learn the language of their playmates.

---

## Activity 1

**On your paper, use these words to complete the sentences below.**

> **communication      gestures      meaning**

- Language involves _____.
- Language sounds must have _____.
- A way of communicating without words is using _____.

Answer the questions under the picture.

1. What is it?
2. How does it communicate?
3. What message does it give?

## Words, Words, Words!

Do you think that words and progress go together? Let's explore this question.

In order to express our thoughts we need a large supply of words. Throughout history, humans have added new words to their languages as they have had new experiences or discovered new things and ideas.

Have you ever considered that scientists and inventors need new words to tell about their discoveries, inventions, and products? So what do they do? They invent new words to go along with their new ideas. For example, *laser, videocassette recorder*, and *modem* are words that have entered English over the last forty years.

How can we keep up with all these new words? We have a special tool. A book that gives word meanings and sometimes tells where each word came from is called a _____. (Check your answer at the bottom of the page.)

dictionary

Have you ever used a dictionary in your classes? Dictionaries contain thousands of words. There are dictionaries for many of the world's languages. Every language consists of words that can be spoken or written. These words, or symbols for ideas, are different in different languages.

## Reading Words

Have you ever stopped to think what a truly wonderful thing it is to be able to read?

What do you do when you read? You look at the words on the page. Those symbols or signs called words have meaning for you because you know what each one represents. When you see words that are familiar to you, a certain picture or idea flashes across your mind. The words recall past experiences and so they are understandable to you.

Our ability to get a thought from a printed word and carry it to our minds is one of our most rewarding achievements.

What do you think are the languages on these signs on a street in San Francisco?

*Courtesy of A. Cannon*

---

| **Activity 2** |
| --- |

Think of words that are new in English. Often they are the names of new inventions or devices. Can you name at least five "new" words? What fields do they come from?

## Why Study Other Languages?

We know that there are many languages in the world and that English borrows from them. As we increase our knowledge of the world around us, our stock of words grows.

Languages are powerful tools to help people everywhere understand one another better.

- Studying a foreign language increases our appreciation of other people and their cultures.
- It helps us understand our own language better.
- It will prepare us for wider opportunities in future careers, such as newspaper work, radio and television, science, publishing, travel, business, and industry.

When we can speak another language we are helping our country as well as ourselves. We are breaking through the language barrier!

In this book, you will become acquainted with examples of African, Asian, and European languages, and even the idea of artificial languages invented for global communication.

In our country, there are people of many nationalities and races speaking numerous languages. All these languages contribute to the English language and to the cultural life of our country.

Welcome to the exciting adventure of exploring some of the world's languages, both in "faraway places" and at home!

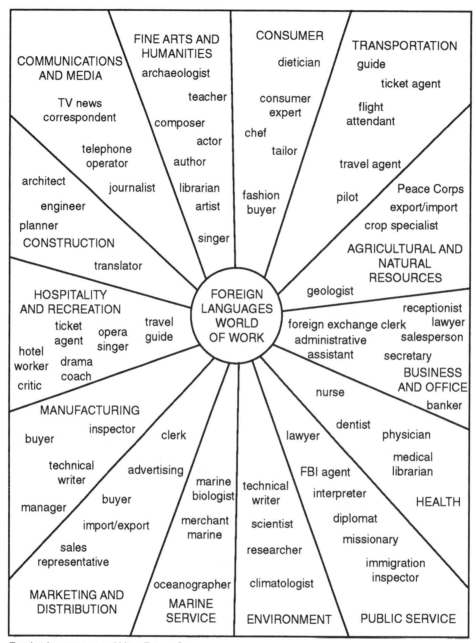

Foreign Languages and Your Future Career

Reproduced with permission, Northeast Conference Reports, p. 129, April 1974

## Activity 3

Interview at least one person who has learned a foreign language. Ask about the advantages of knowing another language. Report your findings to the class.

# C H A P T E R    T W O

# SIGNS AND SYMBOLS*

## Signs of Life

What are symbols or signs and why do we use them? Some signs and symbols convey meaning so clearly that no words are necessary. They are used by all peoples of the world and in all aspects of daily life. Symbols are used as an important part of our communication system.

## Symbols Common in Daily Life

Symbols are signs that are used to represent some object or idea. Words are one example of symbols. Have you seen any other symbols today? Did they stand for several words or even a whole sentence? Symbols that combine several words save both time and space. But

---

*Including Esperanto, an invented language.

even more important is the fact that the symbols are noticed and understood immediately.

Signs and symbols have been used since the cave-dweller days. They were important then and are still important today. Since we live in a fast-paced world, other symbols may often be used in place of words to express ideas and to communicate a message. On television and in store windows, you recognize symbols for foods, clothes, medicine, music, and many other items.

Some symbols represent a language of their own, communication without words. A dollar sign represents money. Even though you may not see the money, you understand what the message is.

Look at the common symbols below. Can you tell what they represent? Investigate those you do not recognize.

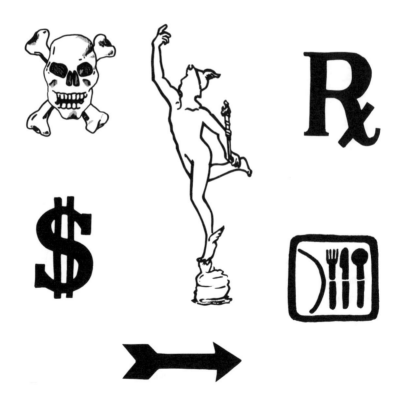

---

### Activity 1

**Can you list, on a sheet of paper, five symbols you recognize that convey a message? Compare your list with that of a classmate.**

## Symbols of Astronomy

The study of the stars and the universe is called astronomy. The science of astronomy uses ancient symbols for the chief heavenly bodies.

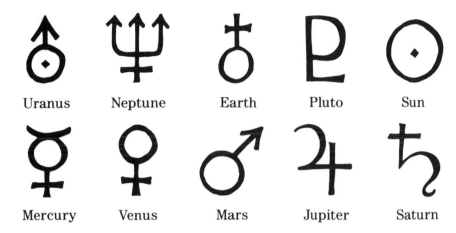

| Uranus | Neptune | Earth | Pluto | Sun |

| Mercury | Venus | Mars | Jupiter | Saturn |

## Mathematical Symbols

What do the following mathematical equations tell us to do?

$2 \times \$1.68 =$
$4 + 3 =$
$6 - 4 =$

Every day we are confronted with mathematical symbols. Our ancestors used symbols to stand for numbers as a means of recording their possessions. The Incas in Peru tied knots in a cord to record each sheaf of grain. Today some people in the world still use the ancient method of cutting a notch in a stick to record numbers.

In our country, we all need to know these common mathematical symbols:

$- + \times \div \% < >$

## Other Signs and Symbols

### Theater
In the theater, a smiling mask stands for comedy; a mask with the corners of the mouth drawn down stands for tragedy. These classic symbols are Greek in origin.

### Science

Scientists from around the world can communicate certain information through the use of common symbols even though they do not speak the same language. The most common formula may be $H_2O$. The $H$ is the symbol for hydrogen and the $O$ for oxygen. The small subscript $2$ signifies two parts of hydrogen to one part of oxygen. Do you know what this symbol stands for in chemistry? It could be ice, clouds, fog, or just plain w _ _ _ r!*

### Cars

The manufacturers of cars often select pictures of animals as symbols to associate power and speed with their cars.

### Countries

Symbols usually appear on the seals of nations or states. These symbols reflect ideas that these nations wish to convey about themselves or their history. The United States seal has an eagle upright, with outspread wings, and an olive branch in its claws.

**Question:**   Can you explain what the United States seal represents and what message it conveys? (Look for this seal in the Latin chapter of this book.)

---

### Activity 2

A.   Select any one of the categories above and bring in information to your class about a sign or symbol that has not been discussed. Bring in a picture or drawing of the sign or symbol.

B.   Identify the well-known symbols below.

---

*Water

### National and International Signs

In many areas of the world there are people who are unable to read or write. A foreigner in a strange country is at a disadvantage because of a lack of knowledge of the language and the country. How would these people get along if there were no common international symbols?

It is important that we familiarize ourselves with the signs and symbols used throughout the world, such as international traffic signs. As the number of automobiles increased throughout the world, the traffic departments of many countries became more safety conscious. International cooperation produced results to benefit everyone.

An American is able to drive a car throughout Europe without fear of misinterpreting road signs because common international symbols are used. As a future driver, it is important for you to learn the language of these international signs. Here are some.

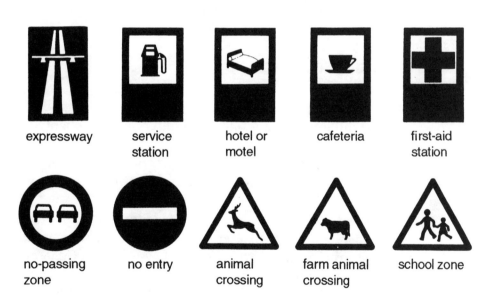

| expressway | service station | hotel or motel | cafeteria | first-aid station |

| no-passing zone | no entry | animal crossing | farm animal crossing | school zone |

# Sign Language

Different forms of sign language are used for communication by deaf persons. This is sometimes called *hand talk*. Using sign language is called *signing*. Scholars believe that signing began in prehistoric times and gradually developed into systems. American Sign Language is just one of the at least fifty sign languages currently used around the world; for example, there is French Sign, Chinese Sign, and German Sign. Do you know someone who knows how to sign? Learning to sign can help you communicate with a deaf classmate or friend. American Sign Language is taught in many schools and colleges.

The art of expressing ideas using hands and fingers is called *gesturing*. Hold up the first two fingers of your hand and you have the "V for Victory" sign made famous by Winston Churchill.* Closing the circle of the thumb and first finger to make an *O* used to be the favorite sign of radio and television producers to indicate that everything on the program was OK. This was in the days before technicians in the broadcast studios wore headphones.

### Braille

A system of raised dots on paper to represent letters and numbers is used for reading by many blind persons. Why is it called Braille [brāl]? (Look this up in an encyclopedia or other reference book.)

## A Hobby That Uses Symbols

Have you ever seen a very high antenna in your neighborhood that seemed different from a television antenna? It probably belongs to an amateur radio operator, or a ham.

Ham radio is one of the most popular hobbies in every country in the world. People of all ages talk to one another either by voice or by Morse Code.**

In order to become a ham in the United States, you have to pass a test for a federal government license. You have to know something about radio electronics and a few important laws. To get a General Amateur License, you still need to know Morse Code. All over the country there are middle school and high school students who are hams. There are even some high school ham clubs. Some astronauts are hams. They have talked to hams on earth while they were in space!

---

*Winston Churchill was the famous prime minister of Great Britain during World War II.

**You may have read about Samuel F. B. Morse in your science or history class. What instrument did he invent? *Hint:* The name comes from the Greek words meaning "faraway writing."

The official name for ham radio is *amateur* radio. No one is sure why the word *ham* came to be used. Can you think of a possible reason? Perhaps in wanting to shorten the word *amateur*, radio operators began saying *h-a-m*.

What language do hams speak when they talk to someone in another country? Hams can have more fun if they know the other person's language! Most hams around the world know some English. There is an international system of letters called Q signals that all hams understand. For example, if a ham sends "QTH?" the receiver knows that he or she is being asked, "Where are you located?" The Q signals are published in a book for hams.

There are many hams in the Caribbean and South America. Hams from the United States can really enjoy communicating with them if they know Spanish! There are some Canadian hams who speak French.

Of course American hams speak to hams in Russia, China, Australia, Japan, and in many other countries throughout the world. Hams like to exchange cards after they have made a contact. These are called QSL cards. Some hams keep all the cards they receive so they have a collection from all over the world.

Here is a real QSL card, reduced in size.

*Courtesy of Dennis Bozeman*

Hams can help people in important ways. They send messages after earthquakes when all other communications have broken down. They can also help communities during hurricanes and floods by maintaining communication within the community and with the rest of the world.

Can you and your classmates think of how the Red Cross and hams work together?

---

### Voice Equivalents on Ham Radio

| | |
|---|---|
| OVER | message sent |
| WAIT | stand by |
| ROGER | message received |
| GO | *all* received |

---

If you would like to find out more about getting a ham license, write to:

American Radio Relay League
Newington, Connecticut 06111

---

### Mystery Word

Ships in distress send the following message by radio:

M A Y D A Y

Find out what the origin of this message is. You will be surprised!

---

## International Morse Code

The Morse code is another method of transmitting messages by radio. It consists of combinations of dots and dashes. The dots and the spaces between the dots and dashes are of equal duration. The dashes are three times as long.

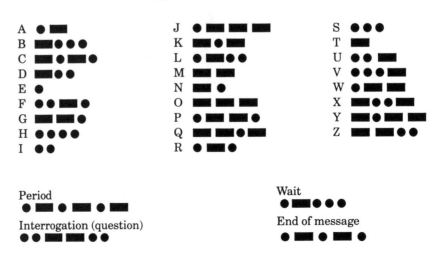

The Morse Code consists of dots and dashes spoken as *dit, dah.*

### International Alphabet for Radio Communication

Hams all over the world agree to use these words when spelling a word in English on voice radio. They use it when they identify themselves.

**Example:** "This is Ted—Tango, Echo, Delta—over."

| | | | |
|---|---|---|---|
| A | ALPHA | N | NOVEMBER |
| B | BRAVO | O | OSCAR |
| C | CHARLIE | P | PAPA |
| D | DELTA | Q | QUEBEC |
| E | ECHO | R | ROMEO |
| F | FOXTROT | S | SIERRA |
| G | GOLF | T | TANGO |
| H | HOTEL | U | UNIFORM |
| I | INDIA | V | VICTOR |
| J | JULIETTE | W | WHISKEY |
| K | KILO | X | X-RAY |
| L | LIMA | Y | YANKEE |
| M | MIKE | Z | ZULU |

▌Activity 3

Compose a message in Morse Code. Be sure to leave spaces between words. Exchange your message with a classmate. Can you read one another's messages?

# An Invented Language

Sometimes, languages are invented to serve special purposes, such as languages to program computers. Invented languages make use of symbols of different types, including letters or number symbols. Have you and your friends ever tried to invent a language so that you could communicate just among yourselves?

From time to time throughout history, people have created languages to help world communication. The idea is that if people in all countries learned a simplified international language in addition to their own language, they would be able to communicate better with one another. It is not intended to replace the study of other languages. The most famous of these invented languages is Esperanto.

Your friends may not have heard about this invented world language. Here are some facts you can share with them.

# Esperanto: What Is It?

1. Esperanto was invented by a young Polish doctor named Ludwig Zamenhof. He first presented it to the public in 1887.
2. The people in his town spoke four different native languages. They often quarreled because they could not understand one another. Some of the people studied the other languages, but that was not enough. To avoid misunderstandings, everyone had to know four languages.
3. Dr. Zamenhof thought, "If people could all speak the same language *in addition to their own language,* perhaps they would not fight so much."
4. He designed Esperanto, using words from Latin, Italian, French, Spanish, German, Polish, and English. He based its name on the Latin verb for *hope—sperare* [spar**ahr**ay].
5. He made it simpler than other languages so it could be learned easily.
6. Now there are people who speak Esperanto in over eighty countries, including the United States.
7. There are more than *five hundred* schools in over forty countries where students take this language in addition to other languages. Thousands of people are studying Esperanto at home.
8. There are Esperanto radio and TV broadcasts in China, Austria, Italy, Spain, Brazil, and other countries.
9. There are about a hundred Esperanto newspapers and magazines, and about thirty thousand books and dictionaries. And the number is increasing.
10. There are organizations for Esperanto in many countries. The main one in the United States is the Esperanto League for North America (ELNA). Esperanto is popular in Europe because so many European countries are surrounded by nations that speak different languages. Esperanto is most popular among the smaller countries whose languages are not studied by many people. You will be surprised to hear which country has the most Esperanto speakers. It is Bulgaria! Find Bulgaria on the map of eastern Europe.

11.  Some people who use Esperanto:
   - scientists
   - stamp and coin collectors
   - international businesspeople
   - chess players
   - computer programmers and hobbyists who communicate around the world
   - worldwide religious organizations
   - ham radio operators
   - international rock groups

12.  Dr. Zamenhof hoped that his language would promote world peace. One of the symbols used by the speakers of Esperanto is the globe surrounded by olive branches. Olive branches stand for peace. (Remember that *Esperanto* means "the language of hope."

D-ro Ludwig Zamenhof, Kriento de Esperanto
(Dr. Ludwig Zamenhof, creator of Esperanto)

*Courtesy of Esperanto League for North America, Inc.; drawing by Laura Dreyer*

Esperanto is officially recognized by the United Nations and by the International Red Cross. By international agreement, it is officially accepted in telegrams around the world.

In 1987, the hundredth anniversary of Esperanto was celebrated at a world conference in Warsaw. The conference was attended by six thousand people. Find Warsaw on the map. What country is it in? Each year there is an Esperanto conference in some city in the world.

Here's something to think about. Would Esperanto be useful to the United States if each state were a different country with its own language?

If you wish to know more about Esperanto, you can write to:

Esperanto League for North America
P.O. Box 1129
El Cerrito, CA 94530

Children around the World (Infanoj Ĉirkaŭ la Mondo)
3876 Belmont Ave.
San Diego, CA 92116
(This organization publishes a student magazine.)

The international organization, the Universal Esperanto Association, has its headquarters in Rotterdam, Holland. There are offices in New York City, Paris, and Beijing, among many others.

## Let's Communicate in Esperanto

Together with a friend try a little Esperanto. Refer to *How It Sounds* to help you with pronunciation. Stress the syllable in heavy type. Try to figure out the meaning before checking the Word Bank.

|  |  | *How It Sounds* |
|---|---|---|
| You: | Saluton! Mia nomo estas [your name]. | Sah**loo**ton! **Mee**ah **no**mo **eh**stahs [your name]. |
| Friend: | Saluton! Mia nomo estas [friend's name]. | Sah**loo**ton! **Mee**ah **no**mo **eh**stahs [friend's name]. |
| You: | Jen pomo. | Yehn **po**mo. |
| Friend: | Dankon. Ĝi estas bongusta! | **Dahn**kon. Jee **eh**stahs bon**goo**stah! |
| You: | Ne dankinde. | Neh dahn**keen**deh. |
| Friend: | Ĝis la revido. | Jees lah reh**vee**do. |
| You: | Ĝis la revido. | Jees lah reh**vee**do. |

### Word Bank

| saluton | hello | nomo | name |
|---|---|---|---|
| mia | my | jen | here is |

| pomo | apple | bongusta | delicious |
|------|-------|----------|-----------|
| dankon | thank you | ne dankinde | you're welcome |
| ĝi | it | ĝis la revido | good-bye |

---

## Activity 4

A.  Make a list of ten words in Esperanto not in the dialogue, together with their translations in English. Look in an encyclopedia or find a book in the library on Esperanto.

B.  People say that many words in Esperanto are similar to words in other languages such as French, Spanish, and German. Find words in these languages that are similar to the words in Esperanto in the dialogue. Ask a school librarian or a language teacher for help.

## Activities and Projects

1.  Look at the names of common symbols. On a piece of paper, draw the symbol associated with each term and explain the meaning of the symbol.

| | |
|---|---|
| Uncle Sam | olive branch |
| lion | alpha and omega |
| horseshoe | peacock |
| X | American eagle |
| skull and crossbones | Smokey Bear |

2.  Bring in a stamp collection. Discuss the significance of the pictures on some of the stamps.

3.  Find out the origin of the signs of the zodiac. People enjoy reading about the sign they were born under, even though they know it is not based on science.

4.  Prepare a report on Louis Braille and his system of reading for the blind. Illustrate the Braille alphabet. You may write to the Columbia Lighthouse for the Blind, 1421 P Street, N.W., Washington, DC, 20005.

5.  Look up the Esperanto movement in an encyclopedia. Create an Esperanto bulletin board for your class.

# YOUR LANGUAGE AND MINE

## AND HOW IT CAME TO BE*

## What Is English?

What is this language known as English? Has it always been spoken by the people who lived in Great Britain? Was it ever different from what it is now? How did so many unusual words get into the language we speak today? Let's see if we can find the answers to these questions.

How did language begin? Was there ever one language that all people spoke? No one has the answers to these questions. We do know that languages have changed throughout history, and that some languages developed from others.

One important language family is Indo-European. Languages from this family are spoken by more than half of the people of the world, including people in Europe and North America. English is an Indo-European language.

*Including place names of our country.

A form of English first developed around 1000 A.D. although you might find it hard to recognize it as English if you saw it written. We do know, however, that the language we speak in America today came from this language spoken on the island of Britain.

Now let us learn some facts about the story of our language—the history of English.

## The Story of English

### Scene 1: The Cave People of Britain

People lived in Britain probably as far back as fifty thousand years ago. By the time of the *Old* Stone Age, they lived in rock shelters or in caves and depended entirely upon animals and on plants that grew wild for food and clothing.

It was during the *New* Stone Age that people began to grow crops. Later, in the Bronze Age, people used metals to make tools. All these were major events in the history of humans.

In the town of Stonehenge, England, are the remains of a mysterious shrine, which was built around 2000 B.C. This was around the end of the Stone Age and the beginning of the Bronze Age. It is a huge circle of tall, flat stones. Scholars are not certain why it was built. Some think it may have been used as a religious center. The stones may have been used to measure the position of the rising sun at special times of the year.

Stonehenge is one of the earliest monuments in what is now England and was built nearly 4,000 years ago. Why it was built remains a mystery.

*Courtesy of the British Tourist Authority*

## Activity 1

Read more about the cave people and report to your class. This may be a group activity. Each member of the group can report on one aspect, for example, food, clothing, family, and so on.

### Scene 2: The Celts Migrate to Britain

By 500 B.C. a group of people migrated to Britain from Europe. These people were called Celts [kĕlts] and their language was Celtic [kĕltik]. At one time, Celtic was an important branch of the Indo-European family, but it is now rapidly disappearing. Traces of it are still to be found in Scotland, Wales, Ireland, and Cornwall.

The Celts were divided into many tribes that fought among themselves. Wells, rivers, and trees were sacred objects to the Celts, and these objects had patron gods and goddesses. The priests of the Celts were called druids.

The Celts knew how to work metal and were skilled in making tools and decorative objects from metals. Celtic art has beautiful patterns made out of simple lines. However, they also used their skills in making weapons, such as swords and spears.

Although the Celts were one of the first people to live in England, their language had little influence on English as we know it today. Practically the only trace of Celtic is in the origin of the names of some places in England; for example, the name *London* may come originally from the Celtic name for the place where the modern city stands.

## Activity 2

A.  Modern Irish, Scottish, and Welsh people are descended from the original Celts. Look at a map of the British Isles to see where these people live.

B.  Do you like to draw? You may wish to draw something made by the Celts, such as a sword or chariot. First you will have to find out what they might have looked like. Check your school library for help. Look for a book on the Celts.

## Scene 3: The Romans Conquer Britain

In A.D. 43, a fleet of Roman ships with 40,000 soldiers landed at the mouth of the Thames River.* At first, the Romans met no enemy, and they marched in from the coast. The Celts hurriedly brought together an army near a river to stop them. The Roman soldiers crossed the river, making a surprise attack. They threw spears and scared the horses pulling the Celts' chariots. In the confusion, the Romans were able to defeat the Celts. The well-trained legions of Rome soon succeeded in conquering all but the farthest corners of the land.

As the Romans advanced, they built forts at important points. They also built roads from the main fort at Londinium to all the other forts. Do you recognize the word *Londinium* as the Latin name for what is now London?

Hadrian's Wall was built by the Romans in the second century A.D. It is one of several remains of the Roman presence in England.

*Courtesy of the British Tourist Authority*

## Scene 4: Hadrian Builds a Wall

Although most of the Celtic tribes were conquered, there were frequent uprisings of the Picts and Scots to the north. These two tribes lived in the highland that the Romans called Caledonia, and

---

*The dictionary shows that the name of this river is pronounced [tĕmz]. What modern city is on this river?

which we now call Scotland. To stop the constant raids of these tribes, Hadrian, who was then the emperor of Rome, decided to build and defend a wall. This famous wall was begun in A.D. 125 and ended the threat of the northern tribes. It was a tremendous building achievement. The wall of stone extended 73 miles and was six feet high and eight feet thick.

---

| **Activity 3** |
| --- |

**Hadrian's Wall still stands today. If you were a tour guide in Britain, how would you describe Hadrian's Wall and its history to a group of tourists from the United States?**

### Scene 5: The Romans Leave Britain

In A.D. 400, barbarians from northern Europe began to threaten the city of Rome. The Roman government brought all of its colonial troops home to protect the city, and so the Roman legions left Britain.

The influence of Latin on the English language can be seen in the names of English towns that end in -*chester*, -*caster*, and -*cester*, such as Dorchester, Lancaster, and Worcester (pronounced [wooster]). These endings come from the Latin word *castra,* which means "camp." These were places where the Roman soldiers set up their camps.

Other interesting word stories from that time:

| | |
| --- | --- |
| *strata via* meant "paved road" | and became the word: *street* |
| *mille passuum* meant "a thousand paces" | and became the word: *mile* |

The greatest influence of the Latin language on English came many years after the invasion of Britain by the Romans. It took place during the 1500s. As scholars studied many new subjects, they found that English did not have the exact words to express these new ideas. Most of the scholars knew Latin, so they began to borrow words from Latin. You can learn more about this in chapter 15.

## Scene 6: Angles, Saxons, and Jutes Come to Britain

When the Roman legions left, the Celts in the south had to protect themselves from the fierce northern tribes. The Celts, weakened after almost four hundred years of domination by the Roman soldiers, decided to ask the Jutes for help. This was a Germanic tribe from the coast of Denmark. With their help the Celts drove the Picts and Scots to the north again. Once in Britain, the Jutes found that they liked the country. The Romans had cleared the woods, established prosperous farms, built excellent roads, and surrounded their forts with small towns. The Jutes came in large numbers and settled the land. Other tribes from Denmark and Germany also came: these were the Angles and the Saxons.

The three Germanic tribes decided to stay. They then sent for more members of their tribes and tried to conquer the Celts. It is during this period that stories were created about the famous King Arthur, who was a Celt. He is supposed to have fought twelve great battles against the fierce tribes who were invading Britain.

## Scene 7: The Roots of English

The Celts were pushed back to Ireland, to Wales, and to a little southwest corner of England called Cornwall. Those Celts who did not withdraw were absorbed by the Angles, Saxons, and Jutes.

The invasion of the Angles, Saxons, and Jutes began between A.D. 400 and A.D. 449, and by A.D. 500 they had completely occupied what is now England. The Angles and Saxons, who were more numerous than the Jutes, settled near the center of the country and quickly assumed leadership. For a long time these Angles, Saxons, and Jutes had separate kingdoms. Finally, a Saxon king called Egbert succeeded in uniting the people.

The Angles, Saxons, and Jutes were Germanic tribes speaking Germanic languages. Because their languages became the foundation of modern English, we say that English is Germanic in origin.

From early in their history, the tribes called their language *Englisc*. Sometime later the country was called *Englaland* (land of Angles). No one can say for sure why the name of the Angles, and not that of the other two tribes, became the name of the country.

## Activity 4

**Find out about King Arthur and his Knights of the Round Table. Can you write a short scene to present to the class about one of the adventures of the king and his knights?**

### Scene 8: Germanic Influence on Our Language

By A.D. 500, the German tribes were settling down and farming their new land. Most of our basic English words dealing with the home and family are of Germanic origin; for example, words such as *house, mother, father.* Many words relating to farming also come from the Angles and Saxons: *earth, wood, field, dog, sheep.*

More important, the German tribes gave us many of the words that are the basic building blocks of English. These are words such as *the, is, there,* and *you.* It is almost impossible to write an English sentence without using one of these short basic words that come from the Angles and Saxons.

Have you wondered where the English names for the days of the week came from? These were the names of gods and goddesses worshiped by the Angles and the Saxons.

- Tuesday—the day of the bravest god, Tiu.
- Wednesday—Woden's day; Woden was the supreme god.
- Thursday—Thor's day; Thor was the god of thunder.
- Friday—Frigg's day; Frigg was the wife of Woden. She was the goddess of marriage.

## Activity 5

**Use an encyclopedia or other reference book to look up:**

- The Germanic goddess of spring (and what holiday was named after her)
- The day of the week named after a Roman god (and what this god was noted for). Might you find this name in a science book? Why?

## Scene 9: The Danes Conquer Britain

About A.D. 700, a tribe from northern Europe known as Danes (and sometimes called Vikings) began to raid the coastal towns of England. They would come upon a town at night, burn the buildings, carry off gold and other treasures, and sail away in their ships.

Let us follow these historical events:

- By A.D. 838, the Danes were beginning to attack some of the towns along the shores of Britain.
- By A.D. 880, much of northeastern England had been conquered and settled by the Danes.
- By A.D. 950, both English and Danes were united under an English king.
- In A.D. 1016, after renewed invasions from Norway and Denmark, the country reunited—this time under a Danish king, Canute.

The Danes and German tribes in England spoke languages that had Germanic roots and that were fairly similar. This helped the two groups to absorb words from each other. Do you think Danish words became a part of English at this time? Of course they did! From the Danes came some of our pronouns: *they* and *she*. In the following activity, you will learn about more words that come from the Danes.

---

## Activity 6

**Figure out the English words that came from the Danes. The definitions for the words are given followed by a clue. Figure out the words and write them on your paper.**

| | |
|---|---|
| above the earth | _ k _ |
| ability gained by practice | _ k _ _ l l |
| what a horror movie does | s c _ r _ |
| an animal of the north | _ e i _ d e _ r |
| covers your body | s _ _ n |
| this has a pane | _ i n d _ _ |

## Scene 10: The Normans Conquer Britain

During the time the Danes were invading Britain, other Vikings, or Norsemen, from the Scandinavian countries came down to the coast of France. They conquered the northern part of that country and lived under the rule of the king of France. These Norsemen came to be called Normans; the section of the country where they lived was called Normandy. Making themselves at home in their adopted country, they learned the French language and adopted French customs. But they retained their fierce, independent, and adventurous spirit. In 1066, William, duke of Normandy, invaded England and defeated the English at the bloody battle of Hastings. The Normans seized all positions of authority. They ruled over England and a large part of France for two centuries!

The Tower of London is one of the great landmarks of Great Britain. Find out about some events that took place there.

*Courtesy of the British Tourist Authority*

## Effect of the Norman Invasion on English

The Norman invasion had a far-reaching effect on English speech and customs. French naturally became the language of the king's court and of high society, although English remained the language of ordinary business. The people who did use English often tried to make it as much like French as possible. They gave some words a French pronunciation and even imitated French spelling. To this day, we use some of these spellings for common words such as *tongue, guilt, guild, guess.* The letter *u* after a hard *g* sound is a French spelling. You may hold the Norman invasion of England responsible for some of the difficulties in spelling English!

Here is a short summary of what happened to English:

1. In 1100 the English language consisted of:
   - A few Celtic words, many of them place names
   - *plus* a few Latin words
   - *plus* the Germanic language brought by Angles, Saxons, and other tribes
   - *plus* the words brought by the Danes

2. In the next three hundred years, at least ten thousand French words were added. Most of these had to do with law, religion, and society.

   Many words that we use commonly today came into English from French during this period. Here are some words dealing with food that came from French into English. Are many of them ones that you use every day?

| | | | |
|---|---|---|---|
| dinner | toast | stew | cream |
| supper | saucer | fry | sugar |
| taste | plate | beef | orange |
| feast | boil | pork | lemon |

3. By 1200 educated people (who in those days were mainly men) in churches and universities knew *three* languages:
   - *English* for everyday living,
   - *French* for social life, and
   - *Latin* for studies. (Remember, French came from Latin.)

During the two hundred years from 1100 to 1300, the English and Normans gradually became one people. English kept its place as the spoken language of the common people, and by the middle of the fifteenth century (1400s), it had regained its place as the official language of the land. During this time the language had changed greatly. Under French influence, it lost its German endings and certain sounds. It adopted a simpler sentence structure. So you can see that our language has a very high percentage of foreign elements!

One of the reasons the language changed so much is that few people ever wrote it. There were no standard forms, and the people were used to many ways of speaking, even many ways of pronouncing the words!

In England in 1476, an Englishman named Caxton set up a printing press. After that, English was spoken the way Mr. Caxton printed it. We say that English started to become *standardized*.

## Words Unlimited

In the United States, our language is based on the English that was spoken during the seventeenth century (the 1600s). That was when the settlement of the American colonies began. Many things have happened to change the English of that day to our modern American English. We are still coining new words, giving new meanings to old words, and adopting words from other languages. The number of words we can produce from our twenty-six-letter alphabet is limitless. Our language has grown to over six hundred thousand words.

## English: Mixture of Languages

Were you surprised to learn that our language is a mixture of many languages? In your ordinary conversation, you constantly use foreign words or words of foreign origin. We call these words *derivatives,* meaning that they have been *derived from,* or come from, words of other languages.

Latin, French, and Anglo-Saxon blended together to provide the basic pattern of the language that we call English. Most of our English words come from Latin and French.

As you study the chapters on languages in this book, you will learn about some words that English has borrowed from other languages. Here are some examples:

| | |
|---|---|
| Spanish | rodeo, fiesta, sombrero |
| French | avenue, ballet, coupon |
| German | kindergarten, delicatessen |
| Italian | balcony, piano, umbrella |
| Arabic | mattress, sofa, syrup |
| Hebrew | amen, cinnamon, sack |

And you will learn about many more such words as you explore the world of languages!

# Place Names in Our Country

You have learned that the English language has words from many languages. Have you ever wondered about the origin of the name of your town or state? Here are some names of places in our country and how they came to be.

Jeri Perkins

## Native American Place Names

The explorers that came to this hemisphere after Columbus heard the names that Native American tribes had given to various locations. The explorers were mainly French, Spanish, and English. As they heard the Native American names, they changed the words to harmonize with the sounds of their own languages.

Some examples of Native American names are:

*Appalachian,* the name of the mountain region, from the Native American word *apalchen* (a Native American village)
*Mississippi,* from *miss* (big) and *sipe* (river)
*Milwaukee,* from *milo-aki* (good land)

## The Great Lakes and Their Region
Most names of the Great Lakes come from Native American words.

**Lake Ontario:** The name was derived from *ontara,* which meant "great lake" in the language of the Huron tribe.

**Lake Huron:** The lake was named Lake of the Hurons for a tribe that was friendly to the French.

**Lake Erie**: The French first called it *Lac du Chat,* meaning "Lake of the Cat," because the Native Americans who lived south of it were known to them as the Cats. The tribe was called "Erieehronons," meaning "panther." The French changed this to *Erie,* which they found easier to pronounce.

**Lake Michigan:** The French first called this the Lake of the Illinois, from a tribe that lived on its western shore. *Illinois* was originally *Iliniwek.* The root of this word, *illini,* means "man." The entire name meant "the tribe of men." Later, the Iliniwek shifted their home to another location. The lake then became *Michiguma,* meaning "big water." In time, it became *Michigan* in English.

**Chicago:** One of the most colorful Native American names is Chicago. Legend has it that the name is derived from a Native American word, *Checagou,* which meant "place of skunk smells." The land at the lower end of Lake Michigan was swampy; many wild onions grew there. The odor given off in the heat of summer would be reason enough to make the Native Americans and the French refer to the place in this way. Some experts believe that the name "Chicago" comes from a Native American word for "strong, powerful."

The names of the Great Lakes have very different origins.

**Wisconsin:** A Native American tribe, the Ojibway, called what is now the state of Wisconsin *Meskousing,* which meant "the meeting place of waters." Let us see how this word became *Wisconsin.* To the French, it sounded like *Ouisconsing.* (Do you know the French word for *yes?* It is *oui* [pronounced "wee"]). When the French said *Ouisconsing,* it sounded like *Wisconsin* to English-speakers.

## French Place Names

As you have just learned, the French explorers had a great deal of influence in naming many of the places in the United States. They took the names from the Native Americans and changed them a bit to make them easier to pronounce.

There are also many places that were named by the French explorers with words from their own language.

**Lake Superior:** This lake was called *Lac Supérieur* by the French, meaning "Upper Lake." The English later adopted this name for the largest of the Great Lakes. Lake Superior happens to be the largest freshwater lake in the world, but it was named for its location at the north of the Great Lakes, not for its size.

**Detroit:** The name comes from the French word *détroit*, meaning "straits." It was given by the French explorers to the river, a narrow strait between two larger bodies of water, Lake Erie and Lake St. Clair. In time, a trading post was established on the banks of the river, and it too was given the name. The name remains today for the city on the site.

**Louisiana:** The French explored the land from the Great Lakes down the Mississippi River. They claimed this land for France, and they named it Louisiana after their king, Louis XIV, the Sun King. The land at the southern end of the French territory keeps the name as the state of Louisiana.

**New Orleans:** This city was the capital of the French colony in the Louisiana territory. It was named after a town in France near Paris called Orléans (pronounced "or-lay-**on**"). New Orleans still has many French influences, including the celebration of Mardi Gras* with a big carnival.

---

*Mardi gras* means "Fat Tuesday." To what does it refer?

## Spanish Place Names

The Spanish explorers named places in several ways.

Look at a map of the United States. Do you see that many places in the Southwest, California, and Texas were named after saints? *San* and *Santa* mean "saint." The Spanish explorers honored their saints by naming their discoveries or settlements and missions after them.

Some place names you can see on a map are San Francisco, Santa Barbara, San Antonio, and Santa Fe. You can find many others.

The Spanish explorers also named places in memory of similar places in Spain, such as the *Sierra Nevada,* a snow-covered mountain range.

Other interesting place names are those that describe something, such as *Boca Raton* (mouth of a rat), *Chula Vista* (a beautiful view), *Escondido* (hidden), and *Los Gatos* (the cats).

Did you ever wonder how Florida got its name? One of the earliest Spanish explorers was Ponce de León. As he explored the coastline of what today is called Florida, he saw that the landscape was rich

The Spanish have left names in several regions of the United States.
Can you think of names to add to the map?

and green with flowers, palm trees, and other tropical plants. Because it was the Easter season, he gave the coast the name *Pascua Florida,* which means "Easter of flowers" in Spanish.

This famous monument, the Alamo, is in San Antonio, Texas. It is one of the places in the U.S. with a name from the Spanish. Find out the history of this monument.

*Courtesy of the Texas Department of Commerce. Tourist Development Agency*

## Our Heritage of English Place Names

The English explorers, like the French and the Spanish, adopted many Native American names. When they landed in a certain place, they learned its name from the tribes who lived there. Most of the Native American words were changed as they passed from one person to another, and in that way became part of the English language.

The English colonists and explorers also enjoyed naming their new settlements after kings, queens, and other famous people, as well as after places in England.

### Virginia

*Virginia* was the first English name given in North America. The area was explored by two English explorers and named *Virginia* in honor of Queen Elizabeth I, who was known as "the Virgin Queen."

## Maryland and Queen Henrietta Maria

King Charles I wanted to honor his wife, Queen Henrietta Maria, by naming an area in the New World after her. So when a new area north of Virginia was being set up as a colony, he bestowed the name *Terra Mariae* on it. This is Latin for "land of Mary," or Maryland.

## What about Pennsylvania?

This area was given to William Penn by the king of England. The king played a joke on Mr. Penn. Mr. Penn suggested the name *Sylvania,* meaning "woodland." The king wrote on the charter "Penn-Sylvania," meaning "Penn's Woodland." The king knew that the religious Penn did not want to name the colony to honor the king or anyone else. Mr. Penn tried to get the name changed back to Sylvania but the king's secretary did not dare contradict what the king had wanted.

There are many more place names in our country with interesting stories. For example, there are Dutch names that have become part of our language. The street Broadway in New York City was called *Breede Wegh* by the Dutch. It was a long path that the Native Americans used on Manhattan Island.

Investigate Wall Street, New York, Harlem, and the Bronx.

Two rivers with Native American names join at this place to form the Ohio River. The city itself is named for a famous English politician of the 1700s. What is the name of the city and the rivers?

*Courtesy of E.D. Kennedy*

## Activity 7

List ten places in the United States whose names interest you. Investigate the origin of each, using encyclopedias and books on place names. Write a report on what you find.

## Mystery Person

Many believe this person was the greatest English writer.
- What is his name?
- What are some of the plays he wrote?

## Topics for Discussion and Review

1. What do we know about the first inhabitants of Great Britain?
2. Who were the Celts? What influence did they have on the English language?
3. Tell about the Roman conquest of Britain. What influence did it have on English?
4. How did the Angles, Saxons, and other tribes help form the English language? Where did these people come from?
5. Give some examples of the Germanic influence on our language.
6. What happened as a result of the Norman invasion of Britain? How did this change English?
7. How has our vocabulary changed from that of the seventeenth century? Why has it changed?
8. What effect did the invention of the printing press have on the English language?

## Activities and Projects

1. Prepare a "fact sheet" to be distributed to your classmates about each of the following:

   Celts                          Angles and Saxons
   Julius Caesar                  William, Duke of Normandy
   King Arthur legends            The Norman Conquest

2. Trace a map of your state. On it, label places of Native American, French, or Spanish origin, or places named by the first English settlers. Indicate the origin of each place name. This may be a bulletin board project for your class.

## Place Names—A Rap Song

Perform this song with some of your classmates.

The U.S.A. has many faces,
From snow-capped mountains to tropical places.
Strange-sounding names from here and there,
From Santa Fe, Monterrey, to Eau Claire.

Baton Rouge means a large red cane.
Say there, buddy, have you ever been to Maine?
I know a place called Pennsylvania,
Don't get it confused with Transylvania.

The Big Apple, New York City,
The Dutch left names that are really pretty.
Brooklyn, Harlem. Yonkers, ooh!
Take the "A" train and enjoy the view.

Detroit, gee, means the "City of Straits,"
Let's go there, for it must be great.
Jamestown, Potomac, and Susquehanna,
Turkey Isle, Stingray Isle, and Urbana.

A few names have been mentioned, it's true.
I can't remember them all, can you?
On behalf of California and Louisiana, too:
Good-bye, farewell, so long, adieu!

—Jeri Perkins

# FAMILIES OF LANGUAGES
## THEIR SIMILARITIES AND DIFFERENCES

## English and Its Relatives

You should not be surprised to learn that the English language has many foreign ancestors and relations. We ought to know something about these relatives of our language. Tracing the "family tree" of English takes us to many places and among many people.

## There Are Many Families of Languages

The languages of the world have been divided into many families or groups. Each language group includes languages that resemble one another in certain ways. For example, here is the word for *mother* in various languages that belong to the same family.

Examples:

mater     mutter     madre     mother

One of the best-known groups of languages is called *Indo-European* (made up of languages spoken from India to Europe). This linguistic family includes English, French, Spanish, German, Italian, Greek, Russian, and the languages of northern India, among others. Between one-third and one-half the world's population speaks languages in this family.

Look at a map of Africa. The *Bantu languages,* spoken in Africa, make up one of the more interesting language families. Look at the areas south of the Sahara Desert. Many of the languages spoken in this area are from the Bantu family—for example, Swahili, Xhosa, and Zulu.

A widely spoken language is Chinese. It belongs to the *Sino-Tibetan* family, which also includes Thai, Burmese, Tibetan, and others. Although the Japanese language has borrowed some Chinese words and characters, it is not part of the same family as Chinese.

In addition to the Indo-European, the Bantu, and Sino-Tibetan language families, there are many others, such as the Ural-Altaic, Southeast Asian, and Austronesian. You may find out more about these in an encyclopedia.

An interesting family is the Sioux language family. Can you think of where these languages are spoken? If you are thinking that it might be in the Great Plains of the United States, you are right. This family includes a group of Native American languages. One of these is Lakota, spoken by Native Americans in the Dakotas.

## Language Trees Have Many Branches

There are sometimes many branches within a family. For instance, the *Indo-European* family tree contains eight branches, as you can see from the picture and this list:

1. Indo-Iranian: Hindi (India), Persian (Farsi) (Iran)
2. Armenian
3. Albanian
4. Greek
5. Italic (Latin): Romanian, Portuguese, Italian, Spanish, French
6. Germanic: English, German, Dutch, Flemish, Swedish, Norwegian, Danish, Icelandic
7. Celtic: Irish, Scottish or Scotch, Welsh, Breton
8. Balto-Slavic: Russian, Bulgarian, Polish, Slovak, Lithuanian

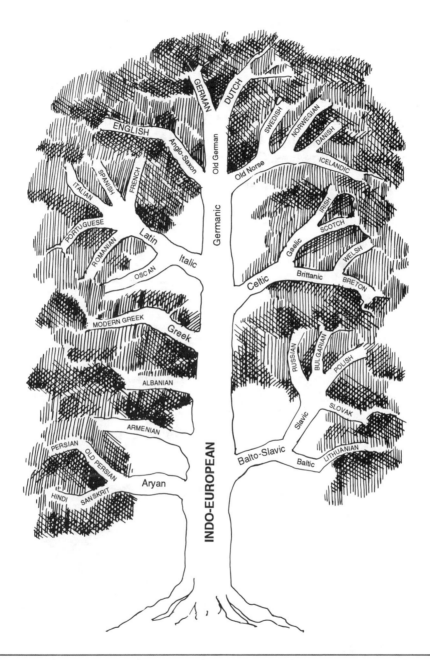

---

## ▍Activity 1

**Choose one of the language families (other than the Indo-European). Use an unabridged dictionary or an encyclopedia (look under *Languages*). Find out the names of some languages in that family. Draw a tree like the Indo-European tree with language branches. Remember that the name of the family should be the trunk of the tree.**

## There Are Many Alphabets

There is no single alphabet for any of the language families. Each language in a group may have a different type of alphabet from the others. Some languages use characters or pictograms instead of letters. Can you name such a language? The Roman alphabet is used for French, Italian, German, Spanish, and many other Indo-European languages. Other alphabets are:

1. the Greek alphabet, used for the Greek language
2. the Cyrillic alphabet, used for Russian and some of the other Slavic languages
3. the Arabic alphabet, used for Arabic, Farsi, and other languages
4. the Hebrew alphabet, used for the Hebrew language. Hebrew is spoken in Israel.

## Activity 2

Study the Indo-European language tree and list three languages that use the Roman alphabet, one language that uses the Greek alphabet, and two languages that use the Cyrillic alphabet. Look up *Cyrillic* in the encyclopedia before listing the languages. Not all the languages in the Balto-Slavic group use this alphabet.

This sign is written in the Roman alphabet. Do you recognize the language of this movie advertisement? Hint: It is from a theater in Madrid.

*Courtesy of Elena Marra-Lopez*

This sign is not written in an alphabet. It is written with characters that stand for
words. Can you guess the language and the language family to which it belongs?
Hint: The sign is in a fish market in Tokyo.

## Languages of the Same Family May Look Alike

We often say such things as "Mary looks like her grandfather,"
meaning that there is a close family resemblance. We can tell
something about the relatives of the English language in the same
way because of the close "family resemblance" among them.

Some scholars of language say that they cannot find features that
are common in *all* the languages of the world. However, they have
found similar root words and similar ways of saying the same thing
in groups of languages. These groups of languages may have had a
common "ancestor" language.

Look at the list below and note the similarities in the words. We
must agree that the likenesses cannot be mere accident. For
example, the English word *mother* looks like Sanskrit *matar*.
(Sanskrit is an ancient language of India.) Read down each column.

| ENGLISH | two | three | mother |
|---|---|---|---|
| DUTCH | twee | drie | moeder |
| GERMAN | zwei | drei | mutter |
| SLOVAK | dva | tri | matka |
| LATIN | duo | tres | mate |
| GREEK | duo | treis | mater |
| SANSKRIT | duva | trayas | matar |

It is largely through comparing words that experts have been able
to write the history of the development of language.

### The Germanic Branch of the Indo-European Tree

For us, the most important branch of our particular language tree is the Germanic, because English belongs to this branch. The reason we say that English is a Germanic language is that our most common everyday words are of Germanic origin.

Here are a few examples:

| English | German | English | German |
|---------|--------|---------|--------|
| come | kommen | milk | Milch |
| drink | trinken | mine | mein |
| hand | Hand | mouth | Mund |

This famous building, the Taj Majal, is in India. What languages are spoken in India?

*Courtesy of A. Cannon*

## Topics for Discussion and Review

1. Give a summary of what you have learned about the Indo-European language family.
2. Why is English called a Germanic language?
3. What language family are you most curious about? Why?

## Activities and Projects

1. Be prepared to explain to the class the language family tree you made in Activity 1 in this chapter. Or ask your teacher to arrange a time for you to explain it to a social studies class.
2. Two *Mystery Words* to investigate and report on to your class: *Creole* and *pidgin*.
3. Investigate and make a chart of some languages that do not use alphabets.
4. Find out about the families of North American Indian languages, such as the Lakota language of the Sioux family.
5. Look up the Greek, Cyrillic, Hebrew, and Arabic alphabets in the encyclopedia. How are they the same? How are they different?

# PART TWO

# Exploring the Languages of the World

# EXPLORING SPANISH
## AND THE HISPANIC WORLD

# ¡Bienvenidos!

## A Romance Language

*Con mucho gusto* is one of the most common expressions in Spanish. It means "with much pleasure," and it is the answer you most often receive when you ask a Spanish-speaking person for any favor—big or small.

Spanish is the language of more than three hundred fifty million people over the world. It is one of the Romance languages. These languages came from Latin, the language of the ancient Romans.

The Romans invaded many areas in Europe and North Africa. One of these areas was the Iberian peninsula. The Romans built cities and towns wherever their armies went. They remained in these places for centuries. The original inhabitants eventually adopted the language of the Romans. The Latin of each area began to change and become different from the others. In Italy, it became Italian; in France, it became French; in Portugal, it became Portuguese; in Spain, Spanish.

This aqueduct, in Segovia, Spain, was built by the ancient Romans.

*Courtesy of A. Cannon*

## Activity 1

**Look at the map in this chapter and find the Iberian peninsula. What countries does it include? Check your answers at the bottom of this page.***

## Spanish-Speaking Countries

The Spanish language has spread to many parts of the world. The Spaniards were among the newcomers to the Western Hemisphere in the 1500s and 1600s. (Remember Columbus and the other explorers who sailed for Spain?) They established colonies, especially in Central and South America, and in much of North America. Of course, they brought their language with them.

*Spain and Portugal

# Map of Spain and the Western Hemisphere

## Activity 2

Spanish is the official language of nine countries in South America. Can you name them? Cover the list and see how many you can name.

| | | |
|---|---|---|
| Argentina | Colombia | Peru |
| Bolivia | Ecuador | Uruguay |
| Chile | Paraguay | Venezuela |

Spanish is also spoken in six Central American countries:

| | | |
|---|---|---|
| Costa Rica | Guatemala | Nicaragua |
| El Salvador | Honduras | Panama |

Buenos Aires, the capital of Argentina, is a beautiful city. Can you find out what the words "buenos aires" mean?

*Courtesy of the Argentine Tourist Office*

## Spanish-Speaking Places Close to Home

Have you ever heard of the "amigo country"? You probably know that *amigo* is the Spanish word for "friend." Some people refer to Mexico, our neighbor to the south, as the "amigo country." Of course, Spanish is spoken there.* Mexicans who are citizens of the United States are Mexican Americans.

Another Spanish-speaking place that is special to the United States is Puerto Rico. Puerto Rico is an island in the West Indies. It used to be a possession of the United States. Since 1952, it has had a special partnership with our country by its own choice. It is called an "associated free state," or the Commonwealth of Puerto Rico. Its people are United States citizens. Look up *Puerto Rico* in an encyclopedia to find out more about this island.

## Activity 3

A.  **Can you name places within our states where people speak Spanish? There are actually millions of Spanish-speaking people who live in the United States. Write the names on a piece of paper.**

B.  **On a sheet of paper, fill in the blanks to complete the words.**

1.  American states that were once part of the Spanish Empire, and later of Mexico.

    C _ _ _ f _ _ _ _ a           T _ _ a _
    Co _ _ r _ d _              New  M _ _ _ c _
    Ar _ _ _ _ a

2.  The southern part of this state became home for thousands of Cubans after Cuba became a Communist country in 1958–60. There are now many Cuban Americans there.

    F _ _ r _ d _

3.  Cities in the United States with large Hispanic populations:

    New  _ _ _ _               C _ i _ ag _
    W _ sh _ _ g _ o _,  D. _.     L _ _  A _ _ e _ _ s
    S _ _  A _ to _ io

---

*When the Spanish conquerors arrived in Mexico and Central America in the sixteenth century, they found advanced civilizations. Investigate the Aztecs and Mayas and the languages they spoke.

Mexico City, the capital of Mexico, is a busy, modern city. This building is the Palace of Fine Arts.

*Courtesy of A. Cannon*

## Circles of Borrowed Words

Can you think of some Spanish words we have borrowed in English?

There are food words from Mexico, such as *tortillas, tacos, burritos,* and *enchiladas.*

Here are circles of borrowed Spanish words. How many words do you recognize?

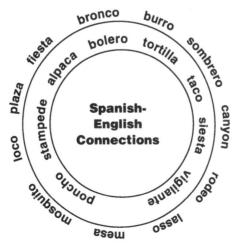

> ### Activity 4

Write definitions of borrowed Spanish words and use them in sentences. You may use the words in the circles or find out about other Spanish words.

## Spanish Pronunciation

The best way to learn to pronounce Spanish is to imitate your teacher and listen to recordings or to people who speak it. Here are a few helpful hints as you listen to and imitate Spanish sounds. Latin American pronunciation is slightly different from that of Spain. Because they are our neighbors, we follow the pronunciation of Latin America.

---

*Vowels:* Do not drag them out; snap them off quickly! Try to pronounce the Spanish examples.

*a* as in *ah* (tortill*a*)
*e* as in p*e*t (m*e*sa)
*i* as in f*ee*t (s*í*)
*o* as in s*o* (*o*cho)
*u* as in f*oo*d (*u*no)

---

*Consonants:* Try to pronounce the Spanish examples.

*d* between vowels: like the *th* in *the* (a*d*iós)
*j:* like *h* (San *J*osé)
*ll:* like *y* (¿Cómo se *ll*ama?)
*ñ:* like *ny* (pi*ñ*ata)
*h:* silent; never sound it! (*h*asta mañana)
*r:* r-r-roll it (Ma*r*ía)
*rr:* r-r-r-roll it even more! (bu*rr*o)

---

As you work in this chapter, you can look at the pronunciation key at the end of the chapter when you need help in pronouncing a Spanish word.

## Activity 5

**On a sheet of paper, match the Spanish words with the meanings listed below. Be sure to:**

- Pronounce the Spanish words correctly.
- Say the words as you practice copying them on your paper.
- Copy each Spanish word twice.

| | | | |
|---|---|---|---|
| adiós | burro | ¿Cómo se llama? | con mucho gusto |
| María | amigo | ocho     piñata | San     sí     uno |

1. eight
2. yes
3. good-bye
4. What's your name?
5. container full of candy and other goodies
6. girl's name
7. one
8. friend
9. donkey
10. saint
11. with much pleasure

### Special Message

For help in finding meanings of Spanish words: Look for a *bilingual* (Spanish and English) dictionary in your class or library.

## The Spanish Alphabet

To use a Spanish-English dictionary, you need to know the Spanish alphabet. Recite the letters on the next page after your teacher. Refer to the pronunciation guide at the end of the chapter.

## El alfabeto

| | | | | | |
|---|---|---|---|---|---|
| a | a | j | jota | r | ere |
| b | be | k | ka | rr | erre |
| c | ce | l | ele | s | ese |
| ch | che | ll | elle | t | te |
| d | de | m | eme | u | u |
| e | e | n | ene | v | ve |
| f | efe | ñ | eñe | w | doble ve |
| g | ge | o | o | x | equis |
| h | hache | pe | y | i | griega |
| i | i | q | ku | z | zeta |

This tower, called La Giralda, is in the city of Seville. Where is Seville?

*Courtesy of A. Cannon*

## Los Números (Numbers)

If you are traveling in a Hispanic area or country, you need to know the numbers for street addresses, prices, bus fares, etc. You must be able to count in Spanish! Here we go . . .

| | | CERO | | |
| | | 0 | | |
| UNO | DOS | TRES | CUATRO | CINCO |
| 1 | 2 | 3 | 4 | 5 |
| SEIS | SIETE | OCHO | NUEVE | DIEZ |
| 6 | 7 | 8 | 9 | 10 |

| | | | |
|---|---|---|---|
| once | 11 | dieciséis | 16 |
| doce | 12 | diecisiete | 17 |
| trece | 13 | dieciocho | 18 |
| catorce | 14 | diecinueve | 19 |
| quince | 15 | veinte | 20 |

Complete the numbers to 30. Write them on a paper to be handed in.

| 21 | veinti*uno* | 26 | veinti*séis* |
|---|---|---|---|
| 22 | veinti*dós* | 27 | _____ |
| 23 | veinti*trés* | 28 | _____ |
| 24 | _____ | 29 | _____ |
| 25 | _____ | 30 | _____ |

*Note:* The words for *22, 23,* and *26* must be written with an accent mark. *Sigamos* ("Let's continue") and count from 30 to 100 by *tens*.

| | |
|---|---|
| treinta 30 (treinta y uno: 31, etc.) | setenta 70 |
| | ochenta 80 |
| cuarenta 40 | noventa 90 |
| cincuenta 50 | ciento 100 |
| sesenta 60 | |

**For eager beavers and word detectives:** What do you think the number *mil* means? *Hint:* Think of *milli*meter!

## Activity 6

**A.** Can you answer *en español?* Write the number words on a sheet of paper.

    1. Half a hundred _____

    2. A dozen _____

    3. Days in a week _____

    4. Number of states in the U.S. _____

    5. Your age _____

    6. Years in a decade _____

    7. Seconds in a minute _____

    8. Students in class today _____

    9. In leap year, February has _____ days.

    Think of at least two more.

**B.** Make up math problems and say them in Spanish. Here are some examples:

    Dos y (+) dos son (=)

    Diez menos (−) cinco son (=)

    Cuatro por (×) cinco son (=)

    Doce dividido por (÷) tres es (=)

---

### Mystery Spanish Word

*Perro* means "dog."
*Perrito* means "little dog."

Surprise! It also refers to something you like to eat. They are very popular at ball games.

*Sign at a ball game in Mexico:*
PERRITOS CALIENTES

What are they?

# Names in Spanish

Let's practice our Spanish pronunciation by learning to say some names of boys and girls. See if you recognize any of these names. Do you see the Spanish form of your own name?

| *Chicos* | *Boys* | *Chicas* | *Girls* |
|----------|--------|----------|---------|
| Alberto | Albert | Alicia | Alice |
| Alfredo | Alfred | Ana | Ann, Anna |
| Andrés | Andrew | Bárbara | Barbara |
| Arturo | Arthur | Beatriz | Beatrice |
| Carlos | Charles | Carolina | Caroline |
| Eduardo | Edward | Dorotea | Dorothy |
| Federico | Frederick | Elena | Ellen, Helen |
| Jorge | George | Leonor | Eleanor |
| Enrique | Henry | Ester | Esther, Hester |
| Juan | John | Florencia | Florence |
| José | Joseph | Juana | Jane, Jean, Joan |
| Pablo | Paul | Lucía | Lucy |
| Pedro | Peter | Margarita | Margaret, Margery |
| Ricardo | Richard | Marta | Martha |
| Roberto | Robert | María | Mary, Marie, Maria |
| Esteban | Stephen | Sara | Sarah |
| Tomás | Thomas | Susana | Susan |
| Guillermo | William | Teresa | Theresa |

# A Few Facts about Names in Spanish

You might be surprised to learn these facts:

- In Spanish-speaking countries, boys and girls are usually named after a saint. The celebration of the feast day of the saint is often considered more important that the person's birthday. It is called *el día del santo* (the day of the saint). For example, all girls named Carmen celebrate their saint's day on July 16. All boys named José celebrate their saint's day on March 19.

- Many boys' names end in *o* and many girls' names end in *a*. This knowledge will help you later in learning about masculine and feminine endings of Spanish words. There are some exceptions. The name Rosario is for a girl.
- When you address a person in Spanish whom you don't know well or talk to a person in authority, you use these words followed by the person's last name:

señor—a man
señora—an older or married woman
señorita—a younger woman

---

| Activity 7 |
| --- |

**Learn the Spanish name of a classmate. Practice saying "Mucho gusto" (pleased to meet you) while you shake hands with him or her and say his or her name.**
   **Example: "Mucho gusto, Juanita."**

## What Time Is It *¿en español?*

¿Qué hora es?

1. Look at each clock face.
2. Look at the Spanish below it.
3. Say the time in Spanish *(en español)*.

Es la una.        Son las cuatro.        Son las seis.        Son las siete.

4. On your paper, draw clocks that have no hands.

5. Draw the hands that tell:
   Son las ocho.
   Son las tres.
6. Draw more clocks.
   Show:
   Son las dos.
   Son las diez.

## Days of the Week *en español (los días de la semana)*

The boys and girls of Spanish-speaking countries use a little rhyme to help them in memorizing the days of the week. You may want to learn it too.

> lunes, martes, miércoles, tres;
> jueves, viernes, sábado, seis;
> domingo, siete

Practice saying the days until you know them.

**Surprise:** The days of the week are not capitalized in Spanish except at the beginning of a sentence.

## Months of the Year *en español (los meses del año)*

Notice that the months resemble the English words in both spelling and pronunciation, but they are not capitalized in Spanish. Pronounce the names of the months after your teacher.

| | |
|---|---|
| enero | julio |
| febrero | agosto |
| marzo | septiembre |
| abril | octubre |
| mayo | noviembre |
| junio | diciembre |

## Activity 8

On your paper, write the name of the month during which each special day falls. Check a calendar if necessary. *¡Escriban en español!*

1. Martin Luther King's birthday
2. School usually begins
3. Christmas
4. The first day of Hanukkah
5. Black History Month
6. Columbus Day
7. First day of spring
8. Mother's Day
9. Father's Day
10. Thanksgiving
11. New Year's Day
12. Halloween

## Using Spanish When Meeting People

People in Spanish-speaking countries use the following expressions to greet each other. Ask your teacher or a friend who speaks Spanish to say these words aloud. Then practice saying them yourself.

| | |
|---|---|
| ¡Hola! | Hi. |
| Buenos días. | Hello. Good morning. |
| ¿Qué tal? | How are you doing? |
| Muy bien, gracias. | Very well, thank you. |
| ¿Y usted? | And you? |

To say good-bye in Spanish, you can use any of these expressions:

| | |
|---|---|
| Hasta la vista. | See you later. |
| Hasta luego. | See you later. |
| Adiós. | Good-bye. |

## Let's Talk *en español*

Juan, one of the Spanish-speaking students in your school, has a friend, Carmen, visiting from Venezuela. Carmen has come to class with Juan. She does not speak English very well. Greet them.

You:    ¡Hola, Juan! ¿Qué tal?
Juan:   Bien, gracias. Quiero presentarte a mi amiga Carmen.
You:    Mucho gusto.
Carmen: Mucho gusto.

### New Words and Phrases

- **Quiero presentarte**   I wish to present to you; I'd like you to meet
- **Mi amiga**   my friend (a girl)
- **Mucho gusto**   Glad to meet you. With much pleasure.

Carmen returns to class the next day. Here's your chance to speak to her.

| | |
|---|---|
| You: | ¡Hola, Carmen! ¿Qué tal? |
| Carmen: | Bien, gracias. Perdón, ¿cómo te llamas? |
| You: | Me llamo _____ (give your name). |
| Carmen: | ¡Mucho gusto! |

### New Words and Phrases

- **Perdón**   Pardon me; excuse me
- **¿Cómo te llamas?**   What is your name?
- **Me llamo ...**   My name is _____.

---

### Activity 9

**Write a minidialogue with one or two partners and present it to the class. Use the phrases you have learned.**

## Using Spanish in Class

Here are some classroom directions for you to recognize and carry out. Try to figure them out before you check their meanings on the next page.

| *To the Class* | *To One Person* |
|---|---|
| 1. Repitan. | 1. Repita. |
| 2. Siéntense, por favor. | 2. Siéntese, por favor. |
| 3. Levántense, por favor. | 3. Levántese, por favor. |
| 4. Escuchen. | 4. Escuche. |
| 5. Silencio. | 5. Silencio. |

Here are the meanings:

1. Repeat.
2. Sit down, please.
3. Stand up, please.
4. Listen.
5. Silence, quiet.

## Classroom Objects

| | | | |
|---|---|---|---|
| la pizarra | chalkboard | el pupitre | desk |
| la ventana | window | el mapa | map |
| la pared | wall | el borrador | eraser |
| la tiza | chalk | el libro | book |
| la silla | chair | el papel | paper |
| la puerta | door | | |
| la bandera de los EE.UU.* | U.S. flag | | |

Dolores Church, Mexico City

*Courtesy of A. Cannon*

---

*The name of our country in Spanish is *los Estados Unidos*. Which word means "States"? Which word means "United"? The abbreviation in Spanish is *EE.UU*. Spanish uses the double *E* and double *U* to show that the words are plurals.

## Classroom Talk

| *Questions* | *Answers* |
| --- | --- |
| 1. ¿Quién sabe? (Who knows?) | Yo sé. (I know.) |
| 2. ¿Dónde está la tarea? (Where's the homework?) | No sé. (I don't know.)<br>Aquí está. (Here it is.) |
| 3. ¿Quién va a la pizarra? (Who's going to the board?) | Él va. Ella va. (*He's* going. *She's* going.) |

# Song

Practice this song in Spanish. You may already know the melody, which appears on the next page.

CIELITO LINDO
Una canción mexicana (A Mexican song)

1.  De la Sierra Morena,
    Cielito lindo, vienen bajando
    Un par de ojitos negros,
    Cielito lindo, de contrabando.

*Chorus:*
¡Ay, ay, ay, ay!
Canta y no llores,
Porque cantando se alegran,
Cielito lindo, los corazones.

2.  Una flecha en el aire,
    Cielito lindo, lanzó Cupido.
    Y como fue jugando,
    Cielito lindo, yo fui el herido.

*(Repeat chorus.)*

3.  Ese lunar que tienes,
    Cielito lindo, junto a la boca,
    No se lo des a nadie,
    Cielito lindo, que a mí me toca.

*(Repeat chorus.)*

Find out what the words *Cielito lindo* mean.

## Cielito lindo

VOCABULARIO:

**alegrar**—to gladden, comfort
**bajar**—to descend
**la boca**—the mouth
**cantar**—to sing
**el cielito**—the darling (coll.)
**el corazón**—the heart
**de contrabando**—stealthily
**no se des**—don't give
**la flecha**—the arrow

**fue**—he was
**fui**—I was
**el herido**—the wounded
**jugando**—playing
**junto**—joined to
**lanzar**—to shoot, launch
**lindo, -a**—pretty
**el lunar**—the beauty spot
**llorar**—to weep

**moreno, -a**—brown
**nadie**—no one
**negro, -a**—black
**los ojitos**—the eyes
**un par**—a pair
**la sierra**—the mountain
**tienes**—you have
**tocar**—to touch
**vienen**—come

*Arranged by Ruth De Cesare*

## Topics for Discussion and Review

1. What is meant by the Romance languages? Name them.
2. With a partner in class:
   a. Discuss why English is spoken in the United States, while Spanish is spoken in Mexico.
   b. Discuss some of the languages spoken in Mexico before it was conquered by Spain.
3. Classify all the countries of North and South America by the languages spoken there.
4. Someone remarks, "I don't think knowing Spanish helps your English. I also do not agree that Spanish fluency can help your career."
   List the arguments you would use to debate this person.

## Activities and Projects

1. Obtain a menu from a Mexican restaurant or from a restaurant that serves dishes of some other Spanish-speaking country. Prepare a bulletin board display listing common dishes and what the dishes are made of. Include appetizing pictures from magazines.
2. Prepare a booklet on these Spanish explorers: Cortés, Balboa, Ponce de León, De Soto. Remember to follow the proper format: title page, table of contents, the report, the bibliography, and an index. Include pictures or drawings.
3. Write a skit with a classmate, using some of the Spanish words and expressions you have learned in this chapter.
4. Design a crossword or word search puzzle using these words: lunes, señor, hola, bien, adiós, mucho, bolero, rodeo, taco, fiesta.
5. Prepare a travel brochure to give to a friend, advertising the Spanish-speaking country that interests you most. Be sure you tell where the country is located and some of its main products and attractions. Write, call, or visit a travel agency in your town. You might also write to the country's embassy in Washington, D.C.

6. Plan to lead a class discussion about Columbus. Cover the following points.
   - What country was he from?
   - Where did he want to go?
   - Where did he really go?
   - What foods were brought to Europe as a result of Columbus's voyages?
   - Debate the questions: Did Columbus really discover a "*New* World"? What happened to the original people that he and other explorers found in this hemisphere?

---

### Mystery Words

Below are some Spanish words used in English.
Find out what they mean and use each one in a sentence.

1. *JUNTA*
   [*hoon*-ta]
2. *GILA* MONSTER
   [*hee*la]
3. *EL NIÑO*
   [*neen*-yo]

*Double Mystery:* POPOCATÉPETL

- From what language is this word?
- *What* is it, and *where* is it?

---

This palace, called el Palacio Real, was built by King Philip II of Spain. Find out more about Philip II.

*Courtesy of Tourist Office of Spain*

# Pronunciation Guide for Spanish

This guide will help in pronouncing the Spanish words in this chapter.

### Numbers (page 59)

uno [**oo**noh]

dos [dohs]

tres [trace]

cuatro [**qwah**troh]

cinco [**seen**koh]

seis [**say**ees]

siete [**seeay**tay]

ocho [**oh**choh]

nueve [**nway**vay]

diez [deeace]

once [**ohn**say]

doce [**doh**say]

trece [**tray**say]

catorce [**kator**say]

quince [**keen**say]

dieciséis [deeace ee **say**ees]

diecisiete [deeace ee **seeay**tay]

dieciocho [deeace ee **oh**choh]

diecinueve [deeace ee **nway**vay]

veinte [**vay**eentay]

veintiuno [vayeentee**oo**noh]

veintidós [vayeentee**dohs**]

veintitrés [vayeentee**trace**]

veinticuatro [vayeentee**qwah**troh]

veinticinco [vayeentee**seen**koh]

veintiséis [vayeentee**say**ees]

veintisiete [vayeentee**seeay**tay]

veintiocho [vayeentee**oh**choh]

veintinueve [vayeentee**nway**vay]

treinta [**tray**eentah]

cuarenta [qwah**rehn**tah]

cincuenta [seen**qwehn**tah]

sesenta [se**sehn**tah]

setenta [se**tehn**tah]

ochenta [o**chehn**tah]

noventa [no**vehn**tah]

ciento [**syehn**toh]

### Alphabet (page 58)

| | | | | | |
|---|---|---|---|---|---|
| a | [ah] | j | [**hot**ah] | r | [**ehr**eh] |
| b | [bay] | k | [kah] | rr | [**ehr-r-reh**] |
| c | [say] | l | [**ehl**eh] | s | [**ehs**eh] |
| ch | [cheh] | ll | [**ehl**yeh] | t | [teh] |
| d | [deh] | m | [**ehm**eh] | u | [oo] |
| e | [eh] | n | [**ehn**eh] | v | [veh] |
| f | [**ef**eh] | ñ | [**ehn**yeh] | w | [**dohb**leh veh] |
| g | [heh] | o | [oh] | x | [**ehk**ees] |
| h | [**ach**eh] | p | [peh] | y | [ee **greeay**gah] |
| i | [ee] | q | [koo] | z | [**seh**tah] |

### Days of the Week (page 72)

| | |
|---|---|
| lunes | [**loon**ace] |
| martes | [**mar**tace] |
| miércoles | [**meeair**kohlace] |
| jueves | [**hwayv**ace] |
| viernes | [**vyair**nace] |
| sábado | [**sah**bathoh] (*d* = *th* as in *the*) |
| domingo | [doh**meeng**oh] |

### Months of the Year (page 63)

| | |
|---|---|
| enero | [eh**nayr**oh] |
| febrero | [fehb**rehr**oh] |
| marzo | [**mahr**soh] |
| abril | [ah**breel**] |
| mayo | [**mah**yoh] |
| junio | [**hoon**eeoh] |
| julio | [**hool**yoh] |
| agosto | [ah**gohs**toh] |
| septiembre | [sep**tyehm**breh] |
| octubre | [ok**too**breh] |
| noviembre | [noh**vyehm**breh] |
| diciembre | [dee**syehm**breh] |

### Alphabetical List of Key Words and Expressions

adiós [ahthee**ohs**] (*d* = *th* as in *the*)
amiga [ah**mee**gah]
(la) bandera [bahn**dair**ah]
bien [byehn]
(el) borrador [borr-rah**dohr**]
buenos días [**bweh**nohs **dee**ahs]
(el) burro [**boor**-r-roh]
(la) carta [**kahr**tah]
Cielito Lindo [syeh**lee**toh **leen**doh]
¿cómo? [**koh**moh]
¿cómo se llama? [**koh**moh seh **yah**mah]
con mucho gusto [kohn **moo**choh **goos**toh]
¿dónde está? [**dohn**deh ehstah]
es la una [ehs lah **oo**nah]
escuche [ehs**koo**cheh]
(los) Estados Unidos [ehs**tah**thos oo**nee**thohs] (*d* = *th* as in *the*)
gracias [**grah**seeahs]
hasta la vista [**ahs**tah lah **vees**tah]

hasta luego [**ahs**tah **lweh**goh]
hasta mañana [**ahs**tah mahn**yah**nah]
hasta pronto [**ahs**tah **prohn**toh]
hola [**oh**lah]
Juan [hwahn]
levántese [leh**vahn**tehseh]
(el) mapa [**mah**pah]
María [mah**ree**ah]
me llamo [meh **yah**moh]
(la) mesa [**meh**sah]
(el) mesero [meh**seh**roh]
¡mucho gusto! [**moo**choh **goos**toh]
no sé [no seh]
(los) números [**noo**mehros]
(la) pared [pa**rehd**]
perdón [pehr**dohn**]
(el) perro [**pehr**-r-roh]
(la) piñata [pee**nyah**tah]
(la) pizarra [pee**sahr**-r-rah]
(la) puerta [**pwehr**tah]
(el) pupitre [poo**pee**treh]
¿qué hora es? [keh ohrah ehs]
¿qué tal? [keh tahl]
¿quién sabe? [kyehn **sah**beh]
¿quién va . . .? [kyehn vah]
repita [reh**pee**tah]
San [sahn]
sí [see]
señor [seh**nyor**]
señora [seh**nyor**a]
señorita [sehnyor**ee**ta]
siéntese [see**ehn**tehseh]
(la) silla [**see**yah]
son las cuatro [sohn lahs **qwah**troh]
son las seis [sohn las **say**ees]
son las siete [sohn las **seeay**teh]
también [tahm**byehn**]
(la) tarea [tah**rayah**]
(la) tiza [**tee**sah]
y usted [ee **oo**stehth] (*d = th* as in *the*)
(la) ventana [vehn**tah**nah]

# EXPLORING FRENCH
## AND THE
## FRENCH-SPEAKING WORLD

# Bienvenue!

## A Romance Language

*Vive la France!* say the French. "Long live France!" The French are proud of their country and proud of their language. Like English, it is spoken on many continents of the world (including North America, where it is an official language of Canada). French is spoken by more than one hundred twenty million people, and it has given us thousands of English words. People in many countries of the world consider it a mark of distinction to be able to speak French.

Like Spanish, French is one of the Romance languages. As you know, these languages, which grew out of the language of the ancient Romans, began to develop when soldiers and colonists from Rome settled in the places that had been invaded and conquered by the Roman army.

## The Geography of France

On a map of Western Europe, notice the central position of France. This geographic location has been important in the development of French civilization. Find a road map of France and see how Paris naturally serves as the hub, or center, of France. But it is not for the French people alone that Paris is the center of culture, learning, and art. People go there from all over the world to see its magnificent buildings, museums, art galleries, theaters, shops, parks, and boulevards. Many also go there to study art, architecture, music, science, literature, and, of course, the French language.

---

### ▌Activity 1

**Write the answers on a sheet of paper.**

1. Look at the map of France. The river that flows through Paris is called the _____.
2. Name the countries and the bodies of water that surround France.

## France: Its Contributions to the World

French history is full of the names of men and women who have made important achievements, not only for the benefit of their own country, but for the world. How many of these world-famous French names do you recognize? Use an encyclopedia to find out about those you do not know.

*In science:* Ampère,* Lavoisier, Pasteur, Marie and Pierre Curie, Laplace

*In art:* Cézanne, Monet, Matisse, Rodin

*In music:* Bizet, Debussy, Ravel

*Famous French writers:* Voltaire, Rousseau, Hugo

Check your school library for books about France and other famous French people.

---

### ▌Activity 2

**Based on the names mentioned above, research the following clues and figure out the missing identities. Write your answers on a sheet of paper.**

1. He discovered that germs cause disease.
2. He created the famous sculpture *The Thinker.*
3. He wrote *Les Misérables.*
4. Marie Curie discovered _____.

---

*Do you have 20-amp fuses in your house? Find out what this means.

# French around the World

Even though French is an official language of the United Nations, most people associate it only with France. Seldom do they think of other French-speaking regions.

Some of these other French-speaking regions are:

- Algeria, Morocco, Tunisia, the Ivory Coast, Togo, Zaire, Mauritania, Senegal, and a number of other countries in Africa
- Parts of Europe, including Belgium, Switzerland, and Monaco
- Parts of the United States, in areas such as Louisiana and New England
- Several countries in Southeast Asia, such as Vietnam, Cambodia, and Laos
- The large province of Québec in Canada
- Parts of the West Indies, including Martinique, Guadeloupe, and other Caribbean islands
- Islands of the Pacific, such as Tahiti and New Caledonia

These places are shown on the map on page 78.

Do you recognize the building in the background? When it was constructed, the Eiffel Tower was the tallest building in the world.

*Courtesy of the French Government Tourist Office*

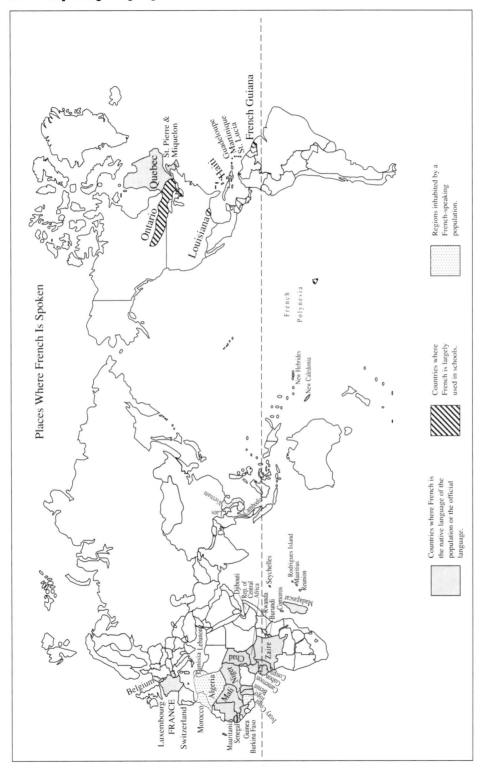

Many people around the world outside of France speak French as a first or second language.

## Canada

In Canada, over 20 percent of the population speaks French. Canada has ten provinces. (Provinces are similar to our states.) The province of Québec has more French-speaking people than any other province in Canada. The most popular places for U.S. students to visit in Québec are the oldest city, Québec City, and the second largest city in Canada, Montréal. There are many small French towns throughout Canada that are dedicated to preserving their French heritage.

Parts of the old town of Québec, Canada, look very much like Europe.

*Courtesy of the Tourist Board, Gouvernement du Québec*

## The French in the United States

There are approximately two million French-speaking people in the United States. They are concentrated mainly in Louisiana, New York, and New England.

In the early 1900s, many French Canadians crossed the border to work in the New England cotton mills and factories. They married Americans, and that is why some New England families have French names and speak French.

The French also influenced other parts of the United States. They were leaders in the early exploration and development of Louisiana, which was named after the French king Louis XIV and purchased from the emperor Napoleon. Some form of French is spoken by many people in Louisiana today. One of these, Creole, is a language derived from French, developed by the descendants of black slaves from Africa who worked in French households.

*Acadian* is the form of the language brought by French settlers who moved to Louisiana from Nova Scotia, Canada. The word *Acadian* became *Cajun*. Do you see the connection? The Cajun people of Louisiana have preserved their music, cuisine, and other customs.

Louisiana has a program to teach modern French to elementary schoolchildren of the state so they will understand their heritage better.

Louisiana is known for its fine Creole and Cajun cooking, and the annual festival called Mardi Gras (which means "fat Tuesday" and which occurs before the period of fasting called Lent).

---

### Activity 3

**Discuss in class French influences in your town, city, or state. For example, do you have an "à la carte" line in the cafeteria at school? Is there a store or restaurant with a French name or menu where you live? Find out if there are French place names with historical significance in your state or region.**

## Borrowings from French

Our own language has been enriched by the thousands of words that we have borrowed from French. If you have read chapter 3, you know why French has a strong influence on English and why so many French words are part of our language.

French has given us many words in art, literature, furniture, dress, textiles, food, clothing, and military science.

| | | | |
|---|---|---|---|
| adieu | buffet | cuisine | naive |
| avalanche | bureau | detour | résumé |
| avenue | cabaret | elite | rouge |
| ballet | chassis | entrée | serge |
| beau | chic | envoy | vogue |
| belle | coupon | façade | |

If some of the above words are new to you, look them up in a dictionary. Use them in a sentence or two; then make them a part of your writing and speaking vocabulary.

French is sometimes used in American advertising. Can you tell what these words mean by their context?

- *Seen on a restaurant menu:*
  SOUP DU JOUR
- *Seen on another restaurant menu:*
  A LA CARTE
- *Seen on a fragrance bottle:*
  EAU de PARFUM
- *Seen on a greeting card:*
  BON VOYAGE

## Activity 4

**Make your own puzzle or word search, using words from the list on the preceding page. Bring them to class. Some may be duplicated for the class to solve.**

## French Pronunciation

The best way to learn to pronounce French correctly is to listen to your teacher or to recordings in your class.

There are many sounds in French that are quite different from any sounds that we have in English. Here are two examples of rounded vowel sounds: The word for "moon" is *lune.* To make the French *u* sound, you should say *ee,* but at the same time pucker your lips as if you were going to whistle. Do the same for the *eu* in the word meaning "fire," *feu,* but make the lips slightly less round and a little more open.

As you study this chapter, you can use the pronunciation guide at the end for help in pronouncing French words.

The Louvre Museum, with its glass pyramid, in Paris, shows the contrast of the old and the new that can be seen throughout France. Research the history of the Louvre.

*Courtesy of the French Government Tourist Office*

# Les Nombres (Numbers)

If you are traveling in France, you will need to know the street number and house number where you are staying. And what about the price of food and taxi or bus fare? You must be able to count in French! Here we go . . .

|  |  | ZÉRO |  |  |
|---|---|---|---|---|
|  |  | 0 |  |  |
| UN | DEUX | TROIS | QUATRE | CINQ |
| 1 | 2 | 3 | 4 | 5 |
| SIX | SEPT | HUIT | NEUF | DIX |
| 6 | 7 | 8 | 9 | 10 |

| onze | 11 | seize | 16 |
|---|---|---|---|
| douze | 12 | dix-sept | 17 |
| treize | 13 | dix-huit | 18 |
| quatorze | 14 | dix-neuf | 19 |
| quinze | 15 | vingt | 20 |

Complete the numbers to 30. Write them on a piece of paper.

| 21 vingt et un | 26 _____ |
|---|---|
| 22 vingt-*deux* | 27 _____ |
| 23 vingt-*trois* | 28 _____ |
| 24 _____ | 29 _____ |
| 25 _____ | 30 trente |

*Continuons* ("Let's continue") and count from 30 to 100 by *tens*.

trente 30 (trente et un: 31, etc.)
quarante 40
cinquante 50
soixante 60
soixante-dix (60 + 10 = _____?)
quatre-vingts (4 × 20 = _____?)
quatre-vingt-dix (4 × 20 + 10 = _____?)
cent 100

## New Words and Expressions

| | |
|---|---|
| Mon numéro de téléphone est . . . | (You are giving your phone number.) |
| Combien? | (You are asking *how much*.) |
| Ça coûte . . . | (You are telling what it costs.) |
| Madame, Monsieur, Mademoiselle | (You would use one of these to address your teacher: *Madame*—an older or a married woman; *Monsieur*—a man; *Mademoiselle*—an unmarried woman. Abbreviations: *Mme, M., Mlle*) |

---

### Activity 5

A. **Read the following telephone numbers in French. Pretend you are in Paris, giving someone a phone number. French phone numbers have eight digits, and the French say them in sets of two digits.**

> Example: 18-12-45-09 would be read *dix-huit, douze, quarante-cinq, zéro neuf.*

> 16-11-15-14
> 20-29-15-10

B. **Your teacher may ask you the price of items that can be bought in the school store or a local drugstore. You should be able to say "ça coûte *soixante* centimes (cents)."**

## Using French When Meeting People

Suppose you are meeting a French-speaking person. Here are some of the words and expressions you will need to exchange greetings. You may want to ask your teacher to say these words aloud for you. Listen carefully, and then say the words yourself.

| | |
|---|---|
| Bonjour. | Hello. |
| Salut. | Hi. |
| Ça va? | Hi, how are things? Is everything OK? |
| Oui. Ça va. | Yes, I am fine. |

| | |
|---|---|
| Très bien, merci. | Very well, thank you. |
| Je vais bien. | I am fine. |
| Comme ci, comme ça. | So-so; OK. |

Here are some words French-speaking people use to say good-bye.

| | |
|---|---|
| Au revoir. | Good-bye. |
| A bientôt. | See you soon. |
| A tout à l'heure. | See you shortly. |

## Let's Talk in French

Once you have started a conversation in French with a new friend, you might like to talk about yourself or introduce someone to your French-speaking friend. Here are some phrases that will help you.

| | |
|---|---|
| Je te présente . . . | May I present . . .? (I'd like you to meet . . .) |
| Comment t'appelles-tu? | What's your name? |
| Je m'appelle . . . | My name is . . . |
| Tu habites à Québec? | Do you live in Québec City? |
| J'habite à . . . | I live in . . . |
| ma sœur | my sister |
| Nous allons au concert. | We're going to the concert. |
| Bon. | All right; OK. |

Your cousin Bob is coming to visit you and is bringing his friend, an exchange student from Québec, Canada. Imagine the scene and role-play it.

| | |
|---|---|
| You: | Salut, Bob! |
| Bob: | Salut, Dwayne! Je te présente Guy Lupin; Guy, voici mon cousin, Dwayne. |
| Guy: | Bonjour, Dwayne. Ça va? |
| You: | Bonjour, Guy. Oui, ça va. |

Your sister Allyson comes in.

| | |
|---|---|
| Allyson: | Salut, Bob! Ça va? |
| Bob: | Oui, ça va. |
| You: | Allyson, je te présente Guy Lupin du Canada. |
| Guy: | Bonjour, Allyson. |
| Allyson: | Bonjour, Guy. Tu habites à Québec? |
| Guy: | Oui. J'habite à Québec. |

| | |
|---|---|
| You: | Nous allons au concert, Allyson. |
| Allyson: | Bon! Au revoir. |
| Boys and You: | A bientôt, Allyson. |

The Musée d'Orsay is one of the many museums in Paris. It is an old railroad station that has been made into a museum.

*Courtesy of the French Government Tourist Office*

## Activity 6

**Write a short dialogue and present it to the class. Use the phrases you have learned.**

## Following Directions in French

Your teacher will say certain commands every day. You will learn to recognize them and carry them out.

| | |
|---|---|
| Fermez la porte. | Close the door. |
| Ouvrez le livre. | Open the book. |
| Levez la main. | Raise your hand. |
| Allez au tableau. | Go to the board. |
| Asseyez-vous. | Sit down. |
| Ecrivez votre nom. | Write your name. |

# Au restaurant

Imagine that your class is planning a trip to a French restaurant. Practice the dialogue below. It will help you communicate in French with the waiter and other people.

Waiter:   Voilà la carte, (monsieur, mademoiselle).
You:      Merci.
Waiter:   Vous désirez?
You:      Je voudrais un croque-monsieur, des frites, un Coca, et une salade niçoise.
Waiter:   C'est tout?
You:      Oui, c'est tout. Merci.

## New Words

| | |
|---|---|
| Voilà . . . | Here is . . . |
| Vous désirez? | You would like? (Your order, please.) |
| Je voudrais . . . | I would like . . . |
| croque-monsieur | ham and cheese on bread dipped in egg batter and grilled |
| des frites | some fries |
| un Coca | a Coca-Cola |
| salade niçoise | salad with olives and tuna |
| C'est tout? | Is that all? |

This French château, or castle, was built during the Renaissance, in the 1550s. It shows the refinement of French architecture of the period.

## Activity 7

French food is famous worldwide for its quality. Find out about popular French dishes and their ingredients. Write a report on what you learn. You may want to get a menu from a local French restaurant.

### A French Menu

**Le Consommé Germiny**
Light chicken and beef soup
with sorrel, egg yolks, and cream

**Le Saucisson de Crustacés**
Cold shellfish sausage made with lobster,
scallop, crab, shrimp, and pistachios,
served with vinaigrette sauce and tomato puree

**Le Granité au Barsac**
Barsac wine sherbet

**Le Tournedos Maison Noir**
Filet mignon in five peppercorns,
cognac and cream sauce, topped with goose liver

**La Salade Composée
selon la Saison**
Seasonal mixed green salad with herbs

**La Tarte Chaude aux
Pommes Acidulées Sauce Abricot**
Hot apple tart served with apricot sauce

**Le Café ou l'Espresso**
Coffee or Espresso

**Les Mignardises**
Assorted Maison Blanche Cookies
Compliments of the Chef

*Courtesy of Maison Blanche, Washington, D.C.*

# Let's Sing in French

## Alouette: A French-Canadian Song

VOCABULAIRE:

l'alouette [f.]—the lark
le bec—the beak
le cou—the neck
le dos—the back

gentil      ⎫
gentille   ⎬ pretty, gentle
les pattes [f. pl.]—feet, paws
plumer—to pluck
la tête—the head

*Arranged by Ruth De Cesare*

2. Je te plumerai le bec (bis)*
   Et le bec (bis)
   Et la tête (bis), Oh—!
   (Refrain)
4. Je te plumerai le cou (bis)
   Et le cou (bis)
   Et les pattes (bis)
   Et le bec (bis)
   Et la tête, (bis),Oh—!
   (Refrain)

3. Je te plumerai les pattes (bis)
   Et les pattes (bis)
   Et le bec (bis)
   Et la tête (bis), Oh—!
5. Je te plumerai le dos (bis)
   Et le dos (bis)
   Et le cou (bis)
   Et les pattes (bis)
   Et le bec (bis)
   Et la tête (bis), Oh—!

*(twice)

This is a song about a bird, a lark. Its feathers are being plucked
from its head, beak, claws, and so on!

## Topics for Discussion and Review

1. In what ways is France's geographic location important?
2. What city in France is its center of culture?
3. Why is it an advantage for us to study French?
4. How did English get so many French words into its vocabulary? Give some examples of words we have borrowed from the French. (Look at chapter 3 for more information.)
5. Discuss the French settlements in the United States. In what areas of our country were French settlers most influential?
6. Where in the United States is French spoken today?
7. Where outside France and North America is French spoken?

## Activities and Projects

1. Tell how three of the following influenced France or the world:

   René Descartes          Claude Debussy
   Joan of Arc             Louis XIV
   Napoléon Bonaparte      William the Conqueror

2. Give a brief biographical sketch of each of the following French explorers and their discoveries in the New World:

   Marquette      Cartier       Cadillac
   La Salle       Champlain

3. Find out about the French holiday that takes place on July 14 and that resembles our Fourth of July. Discuss the historical significance of this important day.

4. Prepare a talk on "A Day in Paris," telling what you would like to see and do there during a one-day visit.

---

### Mystery Words

RENDEZVOUS and MAYDAY

- What do they mean?
- Use each one in a sentence.
- What French expression is the origin of *mayday*?

# Pronunciation Guide for French

This guide will help you pronounce the French words in this chapter.

## Numbers (page 82)

zéro [zay**roh**]

un [uhn*]

deux [duh]

trois [trwah]

quatre [kahtr]

cinq [sehn*k]

six [sees]

sept [seht]

huit [weet]

neuf [nuhf]

dix [dees]

onze [ohn*z]

douze [dooz]

treize [trehz]

quatorze [kah**torz**]

quinze [kehn*z]

seize [sehz]

dix-sept [dees-**seht**]

dix-huit [deez-**weet**]

dix-neuf [deez-**nuhf**]

vingt [vehn*]

trente [trahn*t]

quarante [kahrahn*t]

cinquante [sehn*kahn*t]

soixante [swahsahn*t]

soixante-dix [swahsahn*t-dees]

quatre-vingts [kahtr-vehn*]

quatre-vingts-dix [kahtr-vehn*-dees]

cent [sahn*]

## Alphabetical List of Key Words and Expressions

à bientôt [ah byehn***toh**]

à tout à l'heure [ah toot ah **luhr**]

l'addition [lahdee**seeon***]

allez [**ah**lay]

asseyez-vous [ah**say**ay voo]

au revoir [oh reh**vwahr**]

avez-vous [ahvay **voo**]

bon [bohn*]

bonjour [bohn***zhoor**]

ça va? [sah vah]

Canada [kahnah**dah**]

(la) carte [lah***kahrt**]

(un) Coca [uhn* ko**kah**]

comme ci comme ça [kuhm see kuhm sah]

comment t'appelles-tu? [kuh**mahn*t** tah**pehl** tyu]

---

*The *n** in the sound spelling means that the vowel before the *n* is pronounced through the nose. It is called a nasal vowel. The *n** itself is not pronounced.

(au) concert [oh kohn\***sayr**]
(un) croque-monsieur [uhn\* **krohk**-muhsyuh]
de l'eau [duh **loh**]
du poivre [dyu pwavr]
l'eau minérale [loh meenay**rahl**]
écrivez [aykree**vay**]
et [eh]
fermez [**fair**may]
Guy Lupin [guee lyu**pehn\***]
il est [eel eh]
j'habite [zhah**beet**]
je m'appelle [zhuh mah**pel**]
je te présente [zhuh tuh pray**zahn\*t**]
je vais bien [zhuh vay byehn\*]
je voudrais [zhuh voo**dray**]
levez [luh**vay**]
(le) livre [luh leevr]
ma sœur [mah **suhr**]
madame [mah**dahm**]
mademoiselle [mahdmwah**zel**]
(la) main [lah **mehn\***]
(le) menu [luh muh**nyu**]
merci [mayr**see**]
mon cousin [mohn\* coo**zehn\***]
monsieur [muh**syuh**]
nous allons au concert [nooza**lohn\*** oh kohn\***sayr**]
oui [wee]
ouvrez [**oo**vray]
(la) porte [lah pohrt]
Québec [kay**beck**]
(une) salade niçoise [yewn sah**lahd** nee**swahz**]
salut [sah**lyu**]
tableau [tah**bloh**]
très bien [tray **byehn\***]
tu habites [tyu ah**beet**]
voici [vwah**see**]
voilà [vwah**lah**]
vous désirez [voo dayzee**ray**]

# C H A P T E R    S E V E N

# EXPLORING GERMAN
## AND GERMAN-
## SPEAKING AREAS

# Willkommen!

## Welcome to German

*Viel Glück,* says the German to a friend starting out on a new venture.* "Good luck," we say in English to you starting out on a new language experience.

## German and Germany Today

German is spoken not only in Germany, but also in Austria, Switzerland, Luxemburg, Liechtenstein, and by some people in the neighboring central European countries. The Germanic languages are spoken by millions of people.

Here is a word you can practice easily: The German word for "German" is *Deutsch* [doytch].

---

*\*Viel Glück* sounds like "feel glyuck."

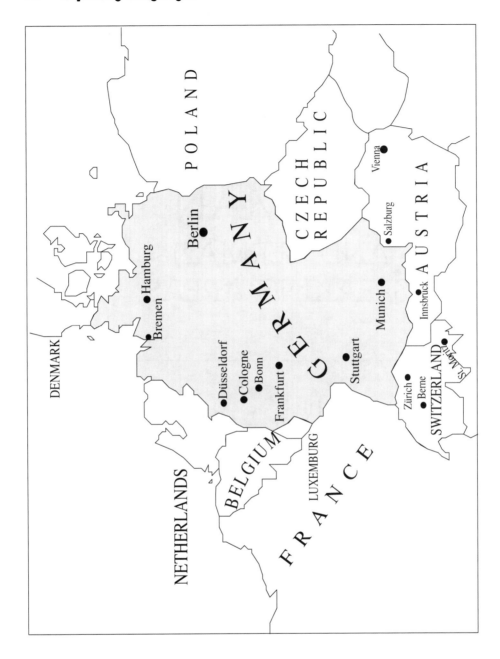

Before World War II, Germany covered an area of 180,000 miles, or roughly two thirds of the area of Texas. After its defeat in the war, Germany was split into separate sections administered by the Allies of World War II: France, Britain, the United States, and the Soviet Union.* These countries had fought against Germany. In 1945, the Soviet part became East Germany and the rest became West Germany.

West Germany had a democratic form of government. Its capital was Bonn. East Germany for many years had a Communist government dominated by the Soviet Union. Its capital was East Berlin.

Check the map in this chapter. You can see that Berlin is on the eastern side of Germany. After World War II, the city was also divided, into East and West Berlin. West Berlin was in the middle of East Germany even though it was part of West Germany.

The city hall of Hamburg, Germany, is a very old, beautiful building. Can you find Hamburg on the map of Germany?

*Courtesy of the German Information Center, Owen Franken, photographer*

---

*Remember that the Soviet Union was a country until 1991. In that year, it broke up into several independent states. Read about this topic in chapter 9, on Russian.

In 1961, the East German government built a twenty-nine-mile wall to keep people from crossing from East Berlin to West Berlin. Many people died while trying to escape to the West. Twenty-eight years later, on November 9, 1989, during demonstrations by thousands of East Berliners, the East Germans opened sections of the wall to let people travel back and forth. Today the wall has been completely torn down. Some people, including Americans, have pieces of the wall as souvenirs. Do you know anyone who has a piece of the Berlin Wall? Ask him or her to tell you about how it was obtained.

The border between the two Germanys was also opened so that people could travel between them.

The four Allied countries of World War II approved the idea of a unified Germany in 1990, and Germany became officially unified on October 3, 1990.

The Berlin Wall, once a symbol of the border between East and West Germany, was dismantled in 1991. Here, the people of Berlin, eager to see their city and country reunited, climb the wall.

*Courtesy of the German Information Center*

## Contributions of German-Speaking People

When you study the German language, you become acquainted with many famous German-speaking people, especially scientists, musicians, writers, and industrialists. Here are some world-famous examples. Have you heard of them before?

### Scientists

Albert Einstein was a professor of physics and one of the world's greatest mathematicians. He became a United States citizen after he left Germany to escape the Nazis in the 1930s.

Wilhelm Roentgen's work with X rays led to the invention of the X-ray machine.

### Writers

Johann Goethe wrote many works. His most famous was a play called *Faust*. Goethe is one of the best-known German writers.

Another name that you might know is that of the brothers Grimm, who wrote the famous *Grimms' Fairy Tales*.

### Musicians

You surely have heard of Bach, Beethoven, and Brahms! Other famous composers include Wagner, Strauss, and Mahler.

From which German-speaking country did Mozart and Haydn come?

### Industrialist

Have you noticed at some gas stations a sign that says "diesel fuel"? The German industrialist Rudolf Diesel invented a motor that runs on fuel oil that is less expensive than the refined gasoline that is needed by most car engines. Diesel engines are used on many trucks. They are also used to generate electric power.

Mercedes-Benz is a German make of car that is sold throughout the world.

*Courtesy of the German Information Center, Owen Franken, photographer*

## Activity 1

Investigate the history of the automobile and the role of Germans in its development. Write a short report and share it with your class.

Name two well-known German cars that we see on American highways. Find pictures of the cars.

## America's Inheritance from the Germans

In the United States today, there are millions of descendants of Germans who came to this country to escape political or religious oppression and economic troubles in Germany. They have made great contributions to our national culture. The "Pennsylvania Dutch"* area in eastern Pennsylvania is primarily German in its background. Many Germans settled there early in our history. They spoke one of the variations of the German language.

There are other areas of the United States where large groups of German-speaking people settled.

## Activity 2

On a sheet of paper, unscramble the names of cities in the United States where the German influence can still be seen.

| State | City |
|-------|------|
| Maryland | eotlbaimr |
| New York | enw kyro yict |
| Ohio | dalcvelne |
| Ohio | nctnniiiac |
| Wisconsin | keeuliwam |

## English and the German Language

Although English got its start from the Germanic languages 1,500 years ago, it still borrows from them. In more recent years, German has given the English language many new words.

---

*Remember the German word for *German?* Do you see that *Dutch* in the term *Pennsylvania Dutch* might really be *Deutsch?*

## Activity 3

Look up these words in a dictionary and find the meaning and history of each one. Write a short composition weaving in these words. It can be serious or humorous.

| | | |
|---|---|---|
| dachshund | kindergarten | strudel |
| delicatessen | Liederkranz | verboten |
| frankfurter | sauerkraut | wanderlust |

**Example**

While I was walking in the city one day, I saw a woman dressed in fancy clothes, walking her *dachshund* on the street. Suddenly she remembered, "Oh, I must go to the *delicatessen;* I forgot my *frankfurters!* And I must pick up my child from *kindergarten.*" As she entered the *delicatessen* she exclaimed, "Oh, my—it smells like *Liederkranz.*" The owner replied, "No, ma'am, you smell *sauerkraut.* Have some!"

## German-English Look-Alikes

Your knowledge of English should help you with German because English is basically very closely related to German. German and English have a great many words so similar that we readily see that they are cognates—that is, related. The word *cognate* comes from the Latin *co* meaning "with" and *natus* meaning "born"; that is, born from the same parent language.

*Ich liebe meine Freunde.** "I love my friends."
Look at the words in the sentence above.
Do you see the words that are similar to English?

Ich       = I
liebe     = love
meine     = my (related to *mine*)
Freunde   = friends

---

*All nouns are capitalized in German.

Look at the names for the days of the week and the months of the year. The connections between German and English are easy to see!

| *Die Tage der Woche* | *Die Monate* |
|---|---|
| Sonntag (Sunday) | Januar |
| Montag (Monday) | Februar |
| Dienstag | März |
| Mittwoch (midweek) | April |
| Donnerstag | Mai |
| Freitag | Juni |
| Samstag/Sonnabend | Juli |
| | August |
| | September |
| | Oktober |
| | November |
| | Dezember |

Liechtenstein Castle is one of the many castles in Germany. They are witnesses to the country's long and varied history.

*Courtesy of the German Information Center*

## Activity 4

Give your new knowledge a try!

Keep in mind all the helpful hints, patterns, and new words you have learned so far, and try to read this brief story about Fritz on your own.

After you read the story, think about what percent of it you understood. Do not peek at the translations until you have determined how much you understood!

## A Story in German

Mein Name ist Fritz Baumgartner. Meine Familie kam aus Deutschland. Mein Vater ist in Hamburg geboren. Meine Mutter ist in Berlin geboren, aber ich bin in Amerika, in Chicago, geboren. Mein Vater und meine Mutter sprechen Deutsch; aber sie sprechen auch Englisch. Ich kann auch Deutsch sprechen; ich lerne Deutsch in der Schule. Ich habe einen Bruder, Heinrich, und eine Schwester, Anna. Mein Bruder ist Student an der Universität Chicago. Er studiert Medizin. Er will Arzt werden. Ich bin im Gymnasium. Ich will nicht auf die Universität gehen.

Did you understand all of the story? How many of the words are similar to words in English?

### Meanings

| | | | |
|---|---|---|---|
| aber | but | kann | can |
| Arzt | doctor | nicht | not |
| auch | also | Schule | school |
| geboren | born | Schwester | sister |
| gehen | go | sprechen | speak |
| Gymnasium | high school | Vater | father |
| kam | came | werden | be |

# A Few Helpful Pronunciation Hints

Even though German and English are alike in many ways, here are some hints for you to follow for those sounds that are different.

### Consonants

*ach* [ahkh] *Bach* [bahkh]

*ich* [eesh or eekh] *ich*

*g* (always hard) *gut*

*j* (always *y* sound) *ja!*

*s* (*z* sound at beginning of word) *sieben*

  (*sh* sound before *t* and *p*) *Strudel*

*sch* [sh] *Schule* [shooleh]

*v* (always *f* sound) *viel!* (much, many)

*w* (always *v* sound) *Willkommen!*

*z* [ts] *zehn, zwei, Heinz*

*ß* (like the *ss* in miss) *muß* (must)

### Vowels

*e* (like *e* in m*e*t) *sechs* (six)
*e, ee, eh* (like *a* in d*a*te) *Beethoven, zehn* (ten)
*ei* (like *i* in l*i*ne) *mein, zwei* (my, two)
*ie* (like *e* in m*e*) *die, sieben* (the, seven)
*eu* (like *oy* in b*oy*) *Deutsch* (German)
*au* (like *ow* in *ow*l) *Frau* (Mrs.)
*u* (like *oo* in m*oo*n) *gut* (good)
*ü* (like *ew* in f*ew*) *über* (over)
*äu* (like *oy* in b*oy*) *Fräulein* (Miss or Ms.)

# Numbers in German

|        |        | NULL<br>0 |       |       |
|--------|--------|-----------|-------|-------|
| EINS   | ZWEI   | DREI      | VIER  | FÜNF  |
| 1      | 2      | 3         | 4     | 5     |
| SECHS  | SIEBEN | ACHT      | NEUN  | ZEHN  |
| 6      | 7      | 8         | 9     | 10    |

| elf      | 11 | sechzehn | 16 |
|----------|----|----------|----|
| zwölf    | 12 | siebzehn | 17 |
| dreizehn | 13 | achtzehn | 18 |
| vierzehn | 14 | neunzehn | 19 |
| fünfzehn | 15 | zwanzig  | 20 |

Complete the numbers to 30. Write them on a paper to be handed in.

| 21 | einundzwanzig | 26 | _____ |
|----|---------------|----|----------------|
| 22 | _____ | 27 | _____ |
| 23 | _____ | 28 | _____ |
| 24 | _____ | 29 | _____ |
| 25 | _____ | 30 | dreißig        |

### Pronunciation Help

| 0 | [noŏl] (like the *oo* in *foot*) | 7 | [**zee**buhn] | 15 | [**fünf**tsayn] |
|---|---|---|---|---|---|
| 1 | [īns] (*ī* as in *eye*) | 8 | [ahkht] | 16 | [**zekh**tsayn] |
| 2 | [tsvī] | 9 | [noyn] | 17 | [**zeeb**tsayn] |
| 3 | [drī] | 10 | [tsayn] | 18 | [**ahkht**tsayn] |
| 4 | [feer] | 11 | [elf] | 19 | [**noyn**tsayn] |
| 5 | [fünf] (*ew* as in *few*) | 12 | [tsvulf] | 20 | [**tsvahn**tsikh] |
| 6 | [zeks] | 13 | [**drī**tsayn] | 30 | [**drī**sikh] |
|   |   | 14 | [**feer**tsayn] |   |   |

## Activity 5

On a sheet of paper, spell out the numbers 22 to 29. Then write the number that tells your age. Write the age of your brother, sister, or friend in German. Make up a number quiz for your classmates.

**Examples:** the number in a dozen, inches in a foot, etc.

The Rhine River attracts thousands of tourists every year. It is also one of Germany's main arteries for transportation of many types of cargo. Find the Rhine on a map of Europe. Why is it geographically important?

*Courtesy of the German Information Center*

## Let's Talk in German!

If some students were to visit your school from Bonn, Germany, how would you greet them? Let's learn some useful phrases to help you get acquainted with someone who speaks German.

Remember that all nouns are capitalized in German.

| German | What It Means | How It Sounds |
|---|---|---|
| Guten Morgen. | Good morning. | [**goo**ten **mor**guhn] |
| Wie geht es Ihnen? | How are you? | [vee **gayt** ess **ee**nuhn] |
| Sehr gut. | Very well. | [zayr goot] |
| Danke schön. | Thank you. | [**dahn**ka shuhn] |
| Und Ihnen? | And you? | [oont **ee**nuhn] |

Say the greetings with a classmate.

# German Food

If you like beef, veal, sausages, potatoes, noodles, breads, and eggs, you might enjoy German dishes. Many of the German specialties are made of these foods.

Hast du Hunger? Are you hungry?

Ja                    oder                    nein?
(Yes)                 (or)                    (no)?

Look at the foods below and tell which one you would select. Guten Appetit!

die Bockwurst (frankfurter/hot dog) [**bock**voorst]

die Milch (milk) [milsh]

die Kekse (the cookies) [**kayk**suh]

der Apfel (the apple) [**ah**pfuhl]

die Trauben (the grapes) [**trow**buhn]

der Fruchtsaft (fruit juice) [**frookht**zahft]

## A Class Trip with a German Bite

You are taking a class trip, and your group is going to eat lunch in a German restaurant. Let's imagine your visit.

| | |
|---|---|
| Waiter: | Guten Tag. |
| You: | Guten Tag. |
| Waiter: | Was möchten Sie, bitte? (What would you like, please?) |
| You: | Haben Sie eine Speisekarte*? (Do you have a set menu?) |
| Waiter: | Ja. (Yes.) |
| You: | Die möchte ich, bitte. (I'd like that, please.) |

## Pronunciation Help

[**goo**ten tak]
[vahs **muhkh**tuhn zee, bittuh]
[**hah**ben zee īnuh **spī**zuhkahrtuh]
[yah]
[dee **muhkh**tuh ish, bittuh]

What are some items that might be on the menu?

| | | |
|---|---|---|
| Gulaschsuppe | [**goo**lahsh **zuh**puh] | thick, spicy beef soup |
| Hamburger | [**hahm**boorger] | hamburger |
| Spätzle | [**shpay**tsluh] | a type of noodle or dumpling |
| Weißbrot | [**vīs**broht] | regular white bread |
| Käseteller | [**kay**zuhteller] | variety of cheeses |
| Tee (oder) Milch | [tay ohder milsh] | tea (or) milk |
| Limo | [**lee**moh] | lemonade |
| Kekse | [**kayk**suh] | cookies |

---

| Activity 6 |
|---|

**Your teacher will help you pronounce the menu items. Design your own menu and write the food names on it. Practice ordering from it.**

---

*German makes words by putting words together. *Speisekarte* is "food card." *Tagesmenü* means "menu of the day." (*Tag* means "day.") Can you figure out what *Tagesuppe* is?

# Let's Sing a German Song

## O Tannenbaum

VOKABELN:

**der Baum**—the tree
**die Beständigkeit**—the constancy
**das Blatt, die Blätter**—the leaf, the leaves
**dein, deine**—your
**dir**—you
**erfreuen**—to give pleasure
**etwas**—something
**gefallen**—to please
**gibt (geben)**—to give
**grünen**—to grow green, flourish
**hat (haben)**—to have
**hoch**—high, a great deal of
**die Hoffnung**—the hope
**im**—in the
**das Kleid**—the dress, garment
**die Kraft**—the strength

**lehren**—to teach, inform
**mir**—me
**nein auch**—but also
**nur**—only
**oft**—often
**schneien**—to snow
**sehr**—very, very much
**sind**—are
**die Sommerszeit**—the summertime
**der Tannenbaum**—the fir tree
**treu**—true, loyal
**der Trost**—the comfort
**von**—from
**die Weihnachtszeit**—Christmas time
**die Zeit**—the time
**zu jeder Zeit**—at all times

Volksweise
*Arr. by Ruth De Cesare*

1. O Tan-nen-baum, o Tan-nen-baum, wie treu sind dei-ne Blät-ter! Du grünst nicht nur zur Som-mers-zeit, nein auch im Win-ter, wenn es schneit. O Tan-nen-baum, o Tan-nen-baum, wie treu sind dei-ne Blät-ter!

2. O Tan-nen-baum, o Tan-nen-baum, du kannst mir sehr ge-fal-len! Wie oft hat nicht zur Wei-nachts-zeit ein Baum von dir mich hoch er-freut. O Tan-nen-baum, o Tan-nen-baum, du kannst mir sehr ge-fal-len!

3. O Tannenbaum, o Tannenbaum, dein Kleid will mich (et)was lehren.
Die Hoffnung und Beständigkeit gibt Trost und Kraft zu jeder Zeit.
O Tannenbaum, o Tannenbaum, dein Kleid will mich (et)was lehren.

*This song is known as the "Christmas tree song." What does the word *Tannenbaum* mean?

## Topics for Discussion and Review

1. Give a report on the history of the "Pennsylvania Dutch" region of the United States.
2. Bring in pictures of German foods and explain how they are prepared.
3. Name three German cars popular in the United States.
4. Name five famous Germans and tell what they are known for.
5. Discuss the role of Germany in World War II.

## Activities and Projects

1. Select a city in Germany to explore. Find out its location, population, six interesting places to see, and a famous person who was born there. Prepare a short report.
2. Have you ever heard of *dirigibles,* or airships? Investigate von Zeppelin and his invention. Tell about the *Hindenburg* disaster.
3. Make a chart for your class bulletin board, showing some of the German words you have learned and their definitions. Make it colorful and interesting!
4. Discuss the various holidays in Germany and tell how they are celebrated.
5. Make an information booklet on one of the following: Austria, Switzerland, Luxemburg, Berlin, or a section of Germany that interests you.
6. Write a report on any of the following topics:

   Mozart
   Lorelei
   the Black Forest
   Oktoberfest
   Grimms' Fairy Tales
   the Berlin Wall
   castles of Germany

## Mystery Words

- *Glockenspiel:* What two German words are in this English word? What do they mean? What does the word mean in English?
- *Kindergarten:* Answer the same questions as above. Why is this word spelled with a *t* instead of a *d*?
- *Blitz:* Have you heard of a media blitz? What is it? What is the German meaning of this word?

# CHAPTER EIGHT

# EXPLORING ITALIAN,
## ITALY, AND ITS PEOPLE

# Ciao!

## Center of the Renaissance

*L'Italia, culla di civiltà,* say the Italians. "Italy, the cradle of civilization." And many would agree that the Italians have a point when it comes to Western civilization.

Even though Italy is somewhat smaller than the state of New Mexico, it has known two periods of greatness and has had an influence far out of proportion to its size.

The first period of greatness happened some two thousand years ago, when Rome was the center of the ancient Western world. Rome dominated most of Europe and parts of the Middle East and North Africa. Rome excelled in art, literature, politics, and building.

The second period of greatness, from the fourteenth century to the sixteenth century, is known as the *Renaissance*. This French word means "rebirth." During this time, the Western world saw much literary and artistic activity, as well as the beginning of modern scientific knowledge. Although the Renaissance had its origins in Italy, its influence eventually spread to most countries in Europe. It marked the shift from the Middle Ages to modern times.

Italians have made great contributions to the world. Here are a few of their names. Look up the ones you do not recognize.

Leonardo da Vinci

Enrico Fermi

Guglielmo Marconi

Alessandro Volta

Galileo Galilei

## The Italian Language

The Italian language is one of the Romance languages, which are all derived from Latin.

You probably already know some Italian words. Read the following passage and see if you can understand what it says.

L'Italia è in Europa. E una penisola. La capitale d'Italia è Roma. Roma è una città antica. La capitale degli Stati Uniti d'America è Washington. Washington non è una città antica.

If you had any trouble understanding the passage, you may need a little help. Read the meanings below only after you have tried to understand the paragraph.

è = is                  di or d' = of
degli = of the          una = a *or* an
una città = a city      antica = ancient

Venice, in northern Italy, is one of the most-visited tourist attractions of the world. Find out why Venice is an unusual city.

*Courtesy of the Italian Government Travel Office*

---

| Activity 1 |
| --- |

**Now try your hand at writing a little Italian. Copy the sentences on a sheet of paper and fill in the missing Italian words.**

1. L'Italia è in _____.
2. L'Italia è una _____.
3. La capitale d'Italia è _____.
4. Washington non è una città _____.
5. Roma è una città _____.

# Greetings in Italian

---

If you were in Italy, you would use the greetings that are shown below. Listen to your teacher pronounce them, and then practice by repeating them several times.

1. Buon giorno!
2. Buona sera!
3. Come stai? Come stai, Carlo? (a friend)
4. Come sta? Come sta, Signora Rossi? (a more formal greeting)
5. Molto bene, grazie.
6. Ciao (or) arrivederci (or) addio.

Glance at the English meanings below to be sure you understand the greetings.

1. Good morning! (or) Hello!
2. Good evening!
3. How are you, Carl?
4. How are you, Mrs. Rossi?
5. Very well, thank you.
6. So long; good-bye.*

## Pronunciation Help

1. buon giorno [bwon **jor**no]
2. buona sera [**bwo**na **say**ra]
3. come stai [**ko**may **stah**yee]

---

*Ciao* can mean "hi" or "so long." *Arrivederci* means "till we see each other again." *Addio* means "good-bye" or "God be with you" (*Dio* means "God").

4. signora [seen**yor**ah]
5. **mol**to bene [**mol**to **bay**nay]
   grazie [**grah**tsyay]
6. arrivederci [ahreevay**dayr**chee]
   addio* [ahd**dee**yo]

---

| Activity 2 |

Use the dialogue below to ask a classmate his or her name and carry on a brief conversation in Italian. If necessary, use the "Pronunciation Help" below.

| | |
|---|---|
| Buon giorno, signore. | Good morning (day), sir. |
| Buona sera, signorina. | Good evening, miss. |
| Come si chiama Lei? | What is your name? |
| Io mi chiamo _____. | My name is _____. |
| Come sta? | How are you? |
| Bene, grazie, e Lei? | Well, thanks, and you? |
| Benissimo, grazie. | |
| Arrivederci! | Till we meet again!/ Good-bye. |
| Buona sera, signora. | Good evening, Madam. |

**Pronunciation Help**

arrivederci [ahreevay**dayr**chee]
buon, buona [bwon, **bwo**nah]
Come si chiama Lei? [**ko**may see **kyah**mah **lay**ee]
giorno [**jor**no]
grazie [**grah**tsyay]
Io mi chiamo [**ee**yo mee **kyah**mo]
Lei [**lay**ee]
sera [**say**rah]
signora [seen**yor**ah]
signore [seen**yor**ay]

---

*Did you know that *good-bye* in English really means "God be with you"?

## Giorni della Settimana (Days of the Week)

Can you recognize these names for the days? You may have guessed that the word *dì* (pronounced *dee*) means "day."

domenica [do**may**neekah]  
lunedì [loonay**dee**]  
martedì [mahrtay**dee**]  
mercoledì [mayrkolay**dee**]

giovedì [jovay**dee**]  
venerdì [vaynayr**dee**]  
sabato [**sah**bahto]

The Trevi is just one of Rome's many beautiful fountains.

*Courtesy of the Italian Government Travel Office*

## Mesi dell'Anno (Months of the Year)

The names of the months come from Latin, like most words in Italian. Practice saying the names with your teacher.

gennaio  
febbraio  
marzo  
aprile  
maggio  
giugno

luglio  
agosto  
settembre  
ottobre  
novembre  
dicembre

## Pronunciation Help for Months of the Year

[jay**nnah**yo] (pronounce both    [**loo**lyo]
*n*s as you would in *penknife*)    [ah**gos**to]
[feb**brah**yo] (pronounce both *b*s)    [set**tem**bray] (pronounce both *t*s)
[**mahr**tso]    [ot**to**bray] (pronounce both *t*s)
[ah**pree**lay]    [no**vem**bray]
[**mahjj**yo] (pronounce both *j*s)    [dee**chem**bray]
[**joo**nyo]

# In Classe (In Class)

Here are some classroom words that are useful to know.

1. il maestro/la maestra    [ma**hay**stro]
2. l'alunno/l'alunna    [a**loon**nah] (pronounce both *n*s)
3. il libro    [**lee**bro]
4. la lavagna    [lah**vahn**yah]
5. il quaderno    [kwah**der**no]
6. il foglio    [**fo**lyo]

Try to get the meanings on your own before checking them below. Read "English Connections" for some help.

## English Connections

1. Have you heard the word *maestro* in English? It usually refers to a symphony conductor.
2. When you graduate from a school, you may join the school's alumni* association.
3. A collection of books is a library.
4. *Folio* (no *g* in English) refers to large sheets of papers used by book publishers.

## Meanings

1. teacher
2. student
3. book
4. chalkboard
5. notebook
6. sheet of paper

*The *alumni* connection is through the original Latin word *alumnus*.

# Numbers in Italian

If you are traveling in Italy, you will need to know the street number and the house number where you are staying. And what about the prices of food and taxi or bus fares? You must be able to count in Italian! Here we go. . .

|  |  | ZERO<br>0 |  |  |
|---|---|---|---|---|
| UNO<br>1 | DUE<br>2 | TRE<br>3 | QUATTRO<br>4 | CINQUE<br>5 |
| SEI<br>6 | SETTE<br>7 | OTTO<br>8 | NOVE<br>9 | DIECI<br>10 |

| | | | |
|---|---|---|---|
| undici | 11 | sedici | 16 |
| dodici | 12 | diciassette | 17 |
| tredici | 13 | diciotto | 18 |
| quattordici | 14 | diciannove | 19 |
| quindici | 15 | venti | 20 |

## Pronunciation Help

In the above numbers, *ci* is pronounced [chee].

| 0-10 | 11-21 |
|---|---|
| [**dzay**ro] | [**oon**deechee] |
| [**oo**no] | [**do**deechee] |
| [**doo**ay] | [**tray**deechee] |
| [tray] | [kwaht**tor**deechee] |
| [**kwaht**tro] | [**kween**deechee] |
| [**cheen**kway] | [**say**deechee] |
| [say] | [deechah**set**tay] |
| [**set**tay] | [dee**chawt**to] |
| [**awt**to] | [dee**chahn**novay] |
| [**no**vay] | [**vayn**tee] |
| [**dyay**chee] | |

Do you see a connection between *dieci* (10) and *-dici* in the teen numbers? For example, *tredici* means "three + ten."

Now you are ready for a challenge. Use the numbers you have learned to make up a telephone number in Italian. Say it to the class to see if they understand.

## Activity 3

**Write these items in Italian:**

- the current month
- the current day of the week
- two things in your classroom
- the number of people in your family

## Italian Musical Terms

One of the largest sources of Italian words adopted by the English language is musical vocabulary. If you examine a piece of music, you will notice that the directions to the musician are given in Italian. For example, if the selection is to be played loudly, it is marked *forte;* if it is to be played softly, it is marked *piano.* All over the world musicians respond to these musical signs in Italian, because they have been adopted by all languages. Look at a piece of music. What does it say to the musician? How is it to be played? To find out, read on.

It is fitting that the world should accept Italian musical signs and terms because of the many Italian contributions to music. Before the seventeenth century (the 1600s), music was printed with only notes; there was no guidance as to speed and force. Then in 1638, an Italian musician named Mazzocchi used terms like *forte, piano,* and *crescendo* when he published some songs. Since Italian music was widely circulated, the words and signs became well known.

## Activity 4

Here are some Italian words that tell musicians what to do when they look at a piece of music. Do you know what these terms mean? Look up any that are unfamiliar to you.

allegro                     staccato
andante                     piano
crescendo                   forte

- How would you play the music if it says *allegro?*
- What is happening in the music if you hear a *crescendo?*
- Use an encyclopedia to find additional terms to add to this list.

Italy also introduced the words *solo, opera,* and *oratorio* to the world of music. Italian opera still occupies a position of great popularity and prominence in opera houses all over the world. Millions of people who do not speak Italian enjoy the beauty of these operas. Some follow the opera's story using a *libretto,* which explains the action. *Libretto* means "little book" in English.

St. Peter's Basilica, in Rome, is the largest church in the world.

*Courtesy of the Italian Government Travel Office*

The city of Florence (Firenze in Italian) is rich in art. Here is the city's government square, or piazza. Find Florence on a map of Italy.

*Courtesy of the Italian Government Travel Office*

## The Birth of a Great Musical Instrument

The word *piano* means "softly" or "slowly." How did it become the name of a world-famous instrument? An Italian, Bartolommeo Cristofori, invented it in 1709. He called his instrument the *stavicembalo col piano e forte*. Unlike earlier keyboard instruments, Cristofori's invention allowed the musician to play either soft *(piano)* or loud *(forte)* tones.

The instrument became known as the *pianoforte*. As more and more people used this word, they shortened it to *piano*.

Would your friends laugh if you asked them, "Do you play the *pianoforte?*"

Do you agree that the word *piano* tells only half the story?

# Classic Italian Song

## Santa Lucia

VOCABOLARIO:

**all'agile**—nimbly
**l'astro**—the star
**la barchetta**—the small boat
**bello**—beautiful
**com' (come)**—how
**con**—with
**così**—thus, so
**d'argento**—made of silver
**luccica (luccicare)**—glitters
**il mare**—the sea
**mia**—my
**la nave**—the ship
**l'onda**—the wave
**il passaggiero**—the passenger

**placido, placida**—calm
**prospero**—flourishing
**questo, questa**—this
**Santa Lucia**—St. Lucy
**soave**—sweet, gentle
**star (stare)**—to stand
**su (venite su)**—(come) aboard
**sul (su + il)**—on the
**sulla (su + la)**—on the
**venite (venire)**—come
**il vento**—the wind
**via**—away
**il zeffiro**—the gentle breeze

*Arranged by Ruth De Cesare*

## Words Borrowed from Italian

In addition to words dealing with music, English has borrowed many other words from Italian. In this section, you'll be learning about the range of words from Italian which add "music" to our language.

---

### Activity 5

**These words have come to us from the Italian language. Look up those you do not know in the dictionary. Then quiz your classmates.**

| | | |
|---|---|---|
| balcony | miniature | sonata |
| bandit | motto | squadron |
| camera | oboe | stanza |
| ditto | opera | stucco |
| fresco | organ | tempera |
| giraffe | piano | trombone |
| macaroni | pizza | umbrella |
| madonna | prima donna | violin |
| maestro | regatta | volcano |

1. What Italian word in this list really means "a room"?
2. What is the Italian word for a picture painted on fresh plaster?
3. What word means "little shade"?
4. Point out all the words having to do with music.
5. Point out the words having to do with art.

## Cibi Italiani (Italian Foods)

- *Italian foods you know about:* pasta, pizza, macaroni, olives and olive oil, spaghetti

- *Maybe you have heard of:* prosciutto, eggplant parmigiana, gelato, lasagne, ravioli, cannelloni, broccoli, garlic, mozzarella, oregano, basil

Below are listed some other everyday foods. Some of the words are very similar to their English equivalents.

| | | | |
|---|---|---|---|
| il pane | bread | le carote | carrots |
| il latte | milk | gli spinaci | spinach |
| l'insalata | salad | i fagioli | beans |
| il formaggio | cheese | la mela | apple |
| il dolce | dessert | l'arancia | orange |
| la carne | meat | la banana | banana |
| il pollo | chicken | l'uva | grape |
| la bistecca | steak | la zuppa | soup |

## Pronunciation Help

| | |
|---|---|
| [**pah**nay] | [lay kah**ro**tay] |
| [**laht**tay] (pronounce both *t*s) | [lyee spee**nah**chee] |
| [insah**lah**tah] | [fa**jo**lee] |
| [for**mahjj**yo] | [**may**lah] |
| [**dol**chay] | [ah**rahn**cheea] |
| [**kahr**nay] | [bah**nah**nah] |
| [**pol**lo] (pronounce both *l*s) | [**oo**vah] |
| [bee**stayk**ka] | [**tsoo**pah] |

# Topics for Discussion and Review

1. Explain why Italy is called "the center of the Renaissance."
2. The *Mona Lisa* is the world's most famous painting. It was painted during the Renaissance period. Find out who painted it.
3. Investigate each of the following Italian personalities. For what achievement is each best known?

   | | |
   |---|---|
   | Columbus | Marconi |
   | Galileo | Garibaldi |
   | Marco Polo | Vespucci |

4. From what language did modern Italian come?
5. Name three contributions Italians have made in the world of music.
6. Name some of the musical terms that have been borrowed from the Italian language.

7.  How many other borrowed words of Italian origin can you think of? List them.
8.  What is your favorite Italian dish? List the ingredients.
9.  Name two fruits in Italian. Name two vegetables.

La Pietà is a famous statue carved by Michelangelo. What do you know about Michelangelo? Look him up in an encyclopedia.

*Courtesy of Maria Wilmeth*

## Activities and Projects

1.  Plan a tour of Italy. Tell the class about the places you would like to visit. Use a wall map of the country to point out the cities, rivers, and mountains on your tour.
2.  Prepare brief biographical sketches of three of the following Italian musicians, telling what each one is famous for:

| | |
|---|---|
| Caruso | Rossini |
| Menotti | Toscanini |
| Puccini | Verdi |

3. Find out about some of the Italian contributions in the field of science and prepare a report for the class. *Hint:* Look in an encyclopedia under *Marconi* and *Fermi.*

4. Go to an art museum in your city or check out a book on paintings from the library. Tell your classmates about some of the Italian paintings and sculptures you saw and give them some information about the most famous Italian artists and sculptors.

5. Tell the class about the explorations of the Italians in the New World. Our country is named after an Italian map-maker. Find out about this man.

6. Prepare a report on some Italian customs, festivals, and holidays.

7. Prepare a scrapbook illustrating various Italian musical terms.

8. Prepare an Italian recipe and share it with your class after you have explained how it was prepared and what ingredients you used.

---

## Mystery Words

1. *Motto.* Maryland is the only state in the United States that has an Italian motto:
   FATTI MASCHII, PAROLE FEMMINE
   - Where did the motto come from?
   - What does it mean?
   - Look up the state of Maryland in the encyclopedia. Look for the meaning of the motto in the article about the state.

2. *Cello.*
   - Where did the motto come from?
   - Do you know someone who plays the *cello* [**chel**lo]?
   - Have you ever gone to a concert where someone played the *cello?*
   - Why is it called a *cello?*

# Mystery Place

What is it? Where is it? What is the Galileo connection?

*Courtesy of the Italian Government Travel Office*

# EXPLORING RUSSIAN,
## RUSSIA, AND ITS PEOPLE

Привет!

## Compact Facts: The Russian Language

Imagine that you are an American student who has been asked to
interview a Russian. By satellite communication, you are talking
with Anna and Ivan (John), two Russian college students. You are
asking some important questions to increase your knowledge about
the Russian language.

Ivan: Hello. In Russian that's Привет [preevyet]. Are you
      ready with your questions?

You: The Russian alphabet is different from the Roman
     alphabet, isn't it?

Ivan: Yes. It's called the Cyrillic alphabet and it has thirty-three letters.

You: Can you tell me something about the history of the Cyrillic alphabet?

Anna: Of course. The Cyrillic alphabet was invented by St. Cyril in the 800s. As you can guess, the alphabet was named after him. When the Slavs who lived in Russia were converted to the Christian religion, they adopted the Cyrillic alphabet.

Ivan: Actually, the Cyrillic alphabet is based mainly on the Greek alphabet, but because the Greek language did not have all the sounds of the Russian language, several letters had to be added to create the Russian alphabet.

You: What other languages use the Cyrillic alphabet?

Ivan: Bulgarian, Ukrainian, and Serbian. These languages are part of the Slavic language family.

You: You mean like Polish?

Anna: Exactly! Polish, Czech, Slovak, Bulgarian—and Russian—are all part of the Slavic language family. Polish, Czech, and Slovak use the Roman alphabet, however.

You: What can you tell me about the Russian language today?

Ivan: About 153 million people speak Russian as their native language. Many more speak it as a second language. It is one of the five most widely spoken languages in the world.

Anna: It is also one of the six official languages of the United Nations.

You: You two speak English very well. Have you studied it for a long time?

Ivan: Yes. In Russia, many students study English beginning in elementary school. Our elementary and high school students attend classes six days a week.

You: Wow, that's a lot of school. Well, it's time to say good-bye. Спасибо [Spah**see**buh]. Thank you. Did I say that right?

Anna: Yes, it was perfect.

Ivan: До свидания [Dah zvee**dahn**yah]. Good-bye!

# Map of Russia

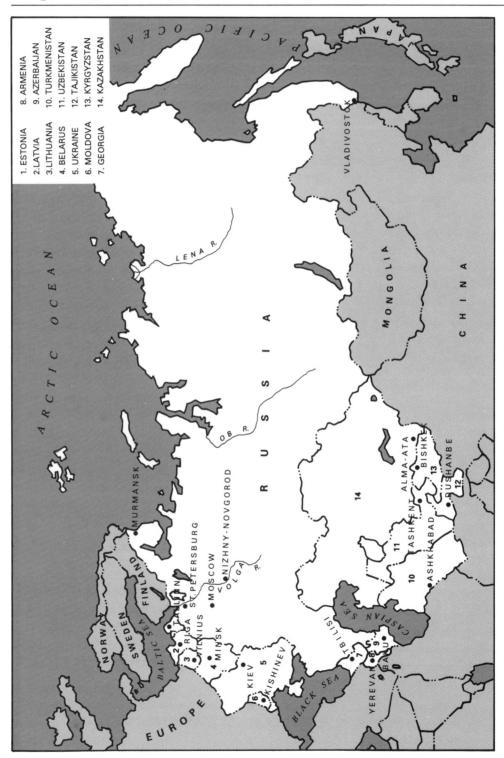

Legend:
1. ESTONIA
2. LATVIA
3. LITHUANIA
4. BELARUS
5. UKRAINE
6. MOLDOVA
7. GEORGIA
8. ARMENIA
9. AZERBAIJAN
10. TURKMENISTAN
11. UZBEKISTAN
12. TAJIKISTAN
13. KYRGYZSTAN
14. KAZAKHSTAN

| Activity 1 |

**Three Russian Words**

| *How It Sounds* | *How It Looks* |
|---|---|
| [pree**vyet**] | Привет |
| [spah**see**buh] | Спасибо |
| [dah zvee**dahn**yah] | До свидания |

Tell what each of the above words means.

In this chapter, you are learning Russian words in *transliterated* form. This means that they are written in the Roman alphabet, not in Cyrillic. In this way, you can become familiar with a few words of Russian even though you can't read the Cyrillic alphabet.

## The Russian Alphabet

There are 33 letters in the Russian alphabet.

| *Russian* | | *Roman Letter(s)* | *How It Sounds* |
|---|---|---|---|
| А | а | a | f*a*r |
| Б | б | b | *b*og |
| В | в | v | *v*ault |
| Г | г | g | *g*o |
| Д | д | d | *d*og |
| Е | е | ye | *ye*t |
| Ё | ё | yo | *ya*wl |
| Ж | ж | zh | a*z*ure |
| З | з | z | *z*one |
| И | и | i | f*ee*t |
| Й | й | y | bo*y* |
| К | к | k | *k*id |
| Л | л | l | *l*aw |
| М | м | m | *m*oose |
| Н | н | n | *n*ot |
| О | о | o | *aw*e |
| П | п | p | *p*ot |
| Р | р | r | th*r*ice (rolled) |
| С | с | s | *s*oot |
| Т | т | t | *t*oe |

| У | у | u | *fool* |
|---|---|---|---|
| Ф | ф | f | *for* |
| Х | х | kh | lo*ch* |
| Ц | ц | ts | i*ts* |
| Ч | ч | ch | *ch*urch |
| Ш | ш | sh | *sch*nauzer |
| Щ | щ | shch | fre*sh ch*eese |
| Ъ | ъ | — | indicates a break for a syllable and hardens a consonant before a y-sound |
| Ы | ы | y, uhy | rh*y*thm |
| Ь | ь | — | usually softens preceding consonant, with attached y-sound, as *n* in canyon |
| Э | э | e | m*e*t |
| Ю | ю | yu | *u*se |
| Я | я | ya | *y*ard |

As you learned from Ivan and Anna, the Russian alphabet is also called the Cyrillic alphabet. Changing a word that is written in one alphabet into another alphabet is called *transliteration*. Let us see why. In Latin, *trans* means "across" and *littera* means "letter" (of the alphabet). We are taking the letters *across* into the other alphabet!

See if you can tell what it is called when we give the meaning of the word in another language.

---

### Activity 2

A.  **Practice pronouncing the name of the Russian alphabet: Cyrillic [sir*i*lic].**

B.  **Look at the Russian alphabet shown and notice letters that look like letters of our own alphabet.**

C.  **Try to write your first or last name in the Russian alphabet. A famous British author, George Bernard Shaw, enjoyed writing his last name in Russian: Шё.**

## A Little Russian History

If you were to continue your interview with Anna and Ivan, you might ask them some questions about Russian history. Here is some of the information they would give you.

St. Basil's Cathedral in Moscow is a popular attraction for visitors.

*Courtesy of Doris Burton*

Russia's history as a country dates back to the years between A.D. 800 and A.D. 900. At that time, the land was inhabited by several Slavic tribes who fought among themselves most of the time. According to legend, they asked a Viking tribe called the Varangian Rus to come and bring order to the region. The Varangian warriors who answered this call were later joined by their families, and the area they settled became known as the land of the Rus.

In the thirteenth century, Russia was invaded by the Mongols. Russia was part of the Mongol Empire, which stretched from China to Europe, until 1480. Russian culture has been greatly influenced by its blend of Asian and European outlooks dating back to this period.

In 1547, Ivan the Terrible was proclaimed the first czar of Russia. Russia was ruled by the czars until the Revolution of 1917.

The workers and common people revolted against the rule of the czars in 1917. The event is known as the October Revolution. It took place on November 7, which was October 25 in the old calendar used in Russia at the time. A group, led by Vladimir Ilyich Lenin, seized power and set up a government on that date. Later, the group took the name of Communists. In 1922, the country became the Union of Soviet Socialist Republics (USSR). It was also commonly called the Soviet Union. Parts of the Russian Empire were broken off to form separate regions called republics, while Russia itself became known officially as the Russian Soviet Federated Socialist Republic. It was the largest of the Soviet republics, covering the majority of the country's territory, and continued to be commonly known as Russia. The word *soviet* means "council." The ruling bodies of the republics were called soviets. Until the end of 1991, there were fifteen republics in the former USSR, each with its own language and culture.

In December 1991, the Soviet Union was officially dissolved. It is no longer one country. The former republics are now independent nations.

## More Compact Facts: Two Important Cities

1. The capital of Russia is Moscow. The people who live in Moscow are called Muscovites. Find out the Russian name for Moscow.
2. The 1980 Summer Olympic Games were held in Moscow.
3. Some famous landmarks in Moscow are:

| | |
|---|---|
| Red Square | the Bolshoi Theater |
| the Kremlin | Moscow University |
| St. Basil's Cathedral | G.U.M. (Moscow's giant department store) |

The Arbat is Moscow's main shopping street. See if you can obtain a street map of Moscow and find Arbat on it.

*Courtesy of Julia Steimel*

4. St. Petersburg is the second largest city in Russia. Could we call it the "on again, off again" city? Notice the march of events.

1703: St. Petersburg is founded by the emperor Peter the Great. Later the city is renamed Petrograd.* Peter makes it the capital of Russia.

1917: The city is renamed Leningrad after the leader of the October Revolution. The capital is moved to Moscow.

1991: The city is renamed St. Petersburg after the residents vote to change the name.

5. St. Petersburg's best-known landmark is the Winter Palace of the empress Catherine the Great. In it is a famous museum with great artworks from all over the world. The name of this museum is the Hermitage.

## Activity 3

**Copy this story on a sheet of paper. Supply the needed words.**

Ivan invited me to visit Russia. The plane I traveled in landed in _____ (the capital city).

I went sightseeing on a bus. I saw a famous theater, the _____, went shopping at _____, and saw a cathedral with domes of beautiful colors, _____.

Write a new story, using additional information. Exchange compositions with a classmate, so that you can read each other's sketches.

### Remember your reference friends

- Encyclopedia
- Dictionary
- Library books on Russia

*Another language connection: the ending, or suffix, *-grad* in Russian means "city." Petrograd means the "city of Peter." Leningrad means the "city of Lenin."

The domes in this photo belong to churches within the walls of the Kremlin. Find out more about the Kremlin.

*Courtesy of Julia Steimel*

## Language Connections

Below are some Russian words you may remember from earlier in the chapter.

| *Russian* | *How It Sounds* | *Meaning* |
|-----------|-----------------|-----------|
| Привет | [pree**vyet**] | _____ |
| Спасибо | [spah**see**buh] | _____ |
| До свидания | [dah zvee**dahn**yah] | _____ |

Look at each Russian word. If you do not remember it, look it up in this chapter. On a sheet of paper, write how each word sounds and its meaning. Here are a couple of easy ones:

| *Russian* | *How It Sounds* | *Meaning* |
|-----------|-----------------|-----------|
| Да | [dah] | yes |
| Нет | [nyet] | no |

Chapter 4, about language families, tells about the Indo-European group. Try to name at least some languages in that group before you look at the bottom of this page.*

---

*Main Indo-European languages: English, French, Spanish, German, Italian, Greek, Russian, Polish, Czech, Slovak, Bulgarian

Look back at the language tree on page 43. When we look closely at the language tree, we see that Russian and English belong to the same large group (Indo-European), but they are not in the same branch. English belongs to the Germanic branch and Russian to the Slavic branch. You should remember that the Romance languages belong to the Italic branch of the Indo-European family.

# English Words from Russian

You are watching a news documentary on Russia with a friend. During the program, you might hear some of the words shown below. Be prepared to explain their meanings to your friend. As you look them up in the dictionary, remember to check the part of the definition that tells the origin of the word.

| | | |
|---|---|---|
| babushka | mammoth | troika |
| balalaika | sable | tundra |
| borscht | samovar | vodka |
| Bolshevik | steppe | |

### Interesting Suffixes
During the documentary, you will probably hear the names of some cities, such as Volgograd. Remember that the suffix -grad means "city."

You have learned babushka, troika, and vodka. The suffix -ka is added to some words in Russian to convey the idea of smallness.

# Let's Talk in Russian

This conversation includes many basic greetings in Russian.

| | *How It Sounds* | *What It Means* |
|---|---|---|
| 1. You: | Preevyet. | Hi! |
| 2. Russian Student: | Kahk vuhy? | How are you? |
| 3. You: | Hahrahsho, spahseebuh. | Fine, thank you. |
| 4. Russian Student: | Kahk vahs zahvoot? | What's your name? |

|  | *How It Sounds* | *What It Means* |
|---|---|---|
| 5. You: | Mee**nyah** zah**voot** _____. Ah **vuhy?** Kahk vahs zah**voot**? | My name is _____. How about you? What is *your* name? |
| 6. Russian Student: | Mee**nyah** zah**voot** Bah**rees**. | My name is Boris. |
| 7. You: | **O**cheen pree**yaht**nah. | Glad to meet you. |
| 8. Russian Student: | **O**cheen pree**yaht**nah. | Glad to meet you. |

*(Shake hands.)*
*(You both must get to class.)*

| 9. Both: | Dah zvee**dahn**yah. | So long! See you later. |
|---|---|---|

Here is the same conversation in the Cyrillic alphabet.

| 1. You: | Привет. |
|---|---|
| 2. Russian Student: | Как вы? |
| 3. You: | Хорошо, спасибо. |
| 4. Russian Student: | Как вас зовут? |
| 5. You: | Меня зовут _____. А вы как вас зовут? |
| 6. Russian Student: | Меня зовут Борис. |
| 7. You: | Очень приятно. |
| 8. Russian Student: | Очень приятно. |
| 9. Both: | До свидания. |

## Activity 4

**A.** Take turns with your classmates role-playing the dialogue. Try to learn the words so that you can say them without looking at the page.

**B.** Writing in Russian

So far in this chapter, we have shown Russian words as they appear in print. When Russians write, they usually do not print. They write in cursive just as we do in English.

Below is the word for "thank you" written in Russian cursive. Practice copying it on your paper.

Keep it as a souvenir of a Russian word you have written!

## Let's Count in Russian

| Russian | Numbers | How It Sounds |
|---------|---------|---------------|
| Один | 1 | [a**deen**] |
| Два | 2 | [dvah] |
| Три | 3 | [tree] |
| Четыре | 4 | [chi**tyr**i] |
| Пять | 5 | [pyaht] |
| Шесть | 6 | [shayst] |
| Семь | 7 | [syem] |
| Восемь | 8 | [**vo**syem] |
| Девять | 9 | [**dyay**vit] |
| Десять | 10 | [**dyay**sit] |

**Fact:** The Russians use the same Arabic numerals for writing as we do. Practice reciting the numbers in order after your teacher. Hold up fingers as you recite. Start with your thumb for *one*.

---

### Activity 5

As a student or your teacher writes numbers at random on the board, say the Russian words. The student or teacher should also write simple addition and subtraction combinations in math symbols to be answered in Russian numbers.

## Russian Arts and Literature

What is a ballet? It is a form of musical entertainment that tells a story through dance.

Two of the world's most famous ballets were written by the Russian composer Tchaikovsky. You probably have seen or at least heard of these masterpieces: *Swan Lake* and *The Nutcracker.*

Russia has produced some of the world's greatest composers.
In addition to Tchaikovsky:

- Rachmaninoff
- Prokofiev*
- Stravinsky

The Bolshoi Theater in Moscow is the world's most famous ballet theater. *Bolshoi* means "big" or "great." *Swan Lake* has been performed at the Bolshoi many times since the first time in 1877.

Many of the world's literary masterpieces came from Russia. You have no doubt heard of some of them; for example, Leo Tolstoy's *War and Peace*. Russian author Boris Pasternak was a winner of the 1958 Nobel Prize in Literature for his book *Doctor Zhivago*.

This picture is from the cover of the program for a
performance at the Bolshoi ballet.

---

*You may be interested in finding out about *Peter and the Wolf,* one of Prokofiev's best-known compositions.

---

**Special United States-Russian
History Connection**

Which of our states was settled by Russian fur traders?
A _ _ _ _ _, the forty-ninth state!
Find out:

- when it was purchased from Russia
- its area (geographically, it is our largest state)
- how far it is from Russia
- what groups of people lived there before it was settled by Russians

---

## The Lighter Side: An Unusual Souvenir

If you visit Russia, you might return with an unusual souvenir: a *matryoshka* doll.

These dolls, called matryoshka dolls, fit one into the other. Find out why they are called matryoshka.

*Courtesy of Charles Gerity*

If you saw brightly painted wooden figures like these, you might not find them unusual—until you take a closer look. They are called "stacking," or "nesting," dolls. One fits into the other down to the smallest one. Some have as many as fifteen or more nesting dolls. As you can imagine, the last one in the stack is extremely small.

Look closely at the word *matryoshka*. Do you see a connection with a Latin word?

Mater (Latin = mother) → Matr-

These nesting dolls are called "mother dolls" by the Russians. Practice pronouncing the word: [matree**yosh**ka].

## Russian Song

# Эй ухнем
## (The Volga Boatmen)

СЛОВАРЬ:

бережок *dim.* (берег)—shore
берёза—birch
ещё разик (раз)—once again
идём (идти)—to go
кудрява (кудрявая)—leafy, bushy (tree)
мы—we
песня—song

по—on
поём (петь)—to sing
раз—time
разовьём (развить)—to show the beauty of
солнышко *dim.* (солнце)—sun
ухнем (ухнуть)—to exert great effort
эй ухнем—yo heave ho

*Arranged by Ruth De Cesare*

Learn to sing the first line.

*Russian transliteration:* **ay**ee **ooh**nyem (repeat)
ye shcho **rahz**eek ye shcho rahz
*In English:* Yo-o heave ho (repeat) once again, one more time

## Russian Review

| How It Sounds | What It Means |
|---|---|
| [pree**vyet**] | Hello. |
| [spah**see**buh] | Thank you. |
| [dah zvee**dahn**yah] | Good-bye. |
| [kahk **vuhy**?] | How are you? |
| [hahrah**sho**] | Well; Fine; OK. |
| [kahk **vahsh**uh **eem**yah?] | What is your name? |
| [kahk vahs zah**voot**?] | What is your name? |
| [ee] | and |
| [mee**nyah** zah**voot**] | My name is . . . |

---

### For Super Sleuths

1. How is the word *czar* used in the United States?
2. Surprise! *Caviar* is *not* a Russian word. Find out what language it comes from and what languages influenced its spelling.

---

## Topics for Discussion and Review

1. Tell the history of the Cyrillic alphabet.
2. Explain why studying Russian is worthwhile. Give examples.
3. To what language family does Russian belong?
4. Below are a few additional words English has borrowed from Russian. Find out their meanings.

   kulak          ukase          Samoyed          kasha

5. Name two Russian composers and two Russian authors.
6. Identify and discuss: *Swan Lake, The Nutcracker, Doctor Zhivago.*
7. Our word for *cosmonaut* is _____.
   From what two languages did the Russians borrow to coin this word?

   cosmos _____ (Language and meaning)
   nauta _____ (Language and meaning)

8. What was known as "Seward's folly" in U.S. history?

# Activities and Projects

1. Prepare a report on the story of the Mongols or on one of their leaders, Genghis Khan.
2. Investigate the Samantha Smith Foundation, Hallowell, Maine, and the summer camp for Russian and American teens. (Find out who Samantha Smith was.)
3. Find out about famous cathedrals in Russia, the colors of their domes, and what is inside them. Explain icons.
4. Find out about the most popular sports in Russia. Compare them with sports in the United States.
5. Prepare a report on the Kremlin. Find out about its history and the purposes it serves today.

---

### For Fun:

Would you like to learn the Cyrillic alphabet? Practice writing your classmates' names and the names of American cities, using the letters on pages 129 and 130. For example, do you know what city this is?

Балтимор

---

### Mystery Word

This is a Russian word sometimes heard in English.

SPUTNIK

What is it?
*Clue:* An important date, October 4, 1957
This is how it looks in Cyrillic:

Спутник

# EXPLORING JAPANESE,
## JAPAN, AND ITS PEOPLE

こんにちは。

## Introducing Japan

Japan is a country of four main islands and thousands of smaller islands. It has approximately 120 million people. Japanese is the official language. Tokyo is the capital. Japan is located in the North Pacific Ocean. Find it on the map.

Between 1638 and 1853, Japan was isolated from other countries. During that time, it became a strongly unified country. Its traditions of strong family units and obedience to older adults were not influenced by the culture of the Western world at that time.

For the Japanese, the *group,* such as the family or the company they work for, is more important than the individual person. How is this idea different from our idea of individual rights and responsibilities?

# Map of Japan

The Golden Pavilion in Kyoto                    *Courtesy of Pat Barr-Harrison*

## Opening to the West

After 1867, Japan's leaders opened their doors to the Western world. They sent many of their young people and scholars to study in other countries.

Japanese industries, railroads, clothing, food, and business came to be influenced by Europe and North America.

On December 7, 1941, Japan bombed Pearl Harbor, Hawaii, and the United States entered World War II. Japan was defeated after almost four years of war.*

After Japan surrendered in 1945, the United States occupied the country and provided money and other resources to help Japan recover. The Japanese economy is now among the strongest and most productive in the world. The Japanese have become leaders in manufacturing products such as television sets, electronics, and cars.

The American occupation helped to strengthen democracy in Japan, even though the Japanese were permitted to keep their emperor as a symbol or figurehead, without real power to rule.

---

*Have you heard of Hiroshima and Nagasaki? These are Japanese cities that were destroyed by American atomic bombs in 1945. The atomic bomb has never again been used anywhere in the world.

## Interesting Facts about Japan

One important city in Japan is Osaka. About one third of the Japanese people live in the area between Tokyo and Osaka. Locate this area on the map.

Japan is traditionally considered a part of the Far East. It might surprise you to know that the Far East lies *west* of the United States!

Modern Japan is an unusual mixture of the old and the new. Ancient traditional festivals and customs exist side by side with the latest in modern technology.

Over 99 percent of the Japanese people can read. Most Japanese believe in the value of an education and in preserving their traditional folk arts and family values.

A very important traditional custom in Japanese culture is the tea ceremony. This ceremony originally came from China. In ancient times in China, tea was used as a medicine and was involved in religious ceremonies. The Japanese borrowed the custom, but they changed it. It is a serious ceremony, but it is also a social time. Formal rules for making, serving, and drinking the tea are carefully followed.

The Japanese have local and national festivals to celebrate many occasions. Most traditional festivals originated as special days to honor a deity* or ancestor, or as agricultural celebrations. There are twelve national holidays in Japan. The most important is Oshōgatsu (New Year's). Homes are decorated. People celebrate and send one another cards.

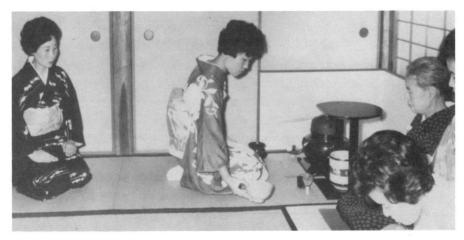

The tea ceremony is an important part of Japanese culture. Find out more about this ceremony.

*Courtesy of Sahomi Sargent*

---

*Deity:* look up this word in your dictionary. It comes from *deus*. What language is *deus*?

## Activity 1

**After reading "Introducing Japan," fill in the missing words. (Write on a sheet of paper, not in this book.)**

1. The _____ ceremony is an important traditional Japanese custom.
2. The capital of Japan is _____.
3. The _____ is more important than the individual in Japanese culture.
4. Japan is made up of _____ main islands.
5. The _____ Ocean is east of Japan, and _____ of the United States.
6. Pearl Harbor is in the state of _____.

# The Japanese Language

Some people may think that the Japanese spoken language is like Chinese. See if you can find the real connection between Japanese and Chinese by reading the information below.

---

*Look for these words as you read:*

| | |
|---|---|
| kanji | kana |
| syllabary | katakana |
| hiragana | romaji |
| ideograms | |

---

### Japanese Language Facts

- Japanese contains many words of Chinese origin even though Japanese and Chinese belong to different language families.
- The Japanese had no system for writing their own language until they began to borrow many Chinese words and *ideograms* about the fourth century A.D. (*Ideograms* are pictures that stand for ideas.)

- The Japanese called the borrowed ideograms *kanji*. They used them to *write* words of their own spoken language. Kanji characters represent whole words. They originally represented pictures of objects or ideas. (*Kanji* means "Chinese letters" in Japanese.)
- They also organized the *sounds* of their language into a written system called *kana*, based on the ideograms. (The word *kana* means "borrowed name.")
- The *kana* system is based mainly on syllables (consonant sound + vowel sound), so it is called a *syllabary* rather than an alphabet.
- There are two groups of *kana: hiragana* and *katakana*. *Hiragana* is used in combination with *kanji* for everyday needs such as in newspapers and textbooks. *Katakana* is used to write foreign words, such as proper nouns and places in other countries. This includes words that the Japanese have borrowed from English and other languages.
- Besides *kanji, hiragana,* and *katakana,* Japanese is sometimes written in the Roman alphabet. This is called *romaji*. (It is used mostly by foreigners, especially when they are trying to learn the language.)

## Activity 2

A.  **Look at the following forms. Try to write them on a sheet of paper. Japanese words are written both *vertically* (up and down) and *horizontally* (across). For vertical writing, the column starts on the right side of the page.**

| English Word | *Kanji Character* | *Hiragana* | *Romaji (Roman alphabet)* |
|---|---|---|---|
| person | 人 | ひと | hito (sounds like [heetoh]) |

Write the *kanji* in the following stroke order:

These students in a Japanese school are practicing writing characters.

*Courtesy of Pat Barr-Harrison*

Write the *hiragana* in the following stroke order:

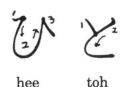

hee        toh

**B.   Discuss with a friend or your class:**

1. Are the Chinese and Japanese languages related?
2. How many writing systems are used by the Japanese?

---

## Did You Know?

- By the time they reach the sixth grade, schoolchildren in Japan must know *hiragana, katakana,* and a good number of *kanji.*
- If Japanese schoolchildren are studying English, they must learn the Roman alphabet too!
- One Japanese sentence can contain words written in *kanji, hiragana,* and *katakana.* In other words, all three writing systems can be used together.

**C.  Which is *hiragana* and which is *kanji*?**

1.    2.

They both stand for:

*English*                     *romaji*
fish                          sa ka na

## Let's Learn a Few Japanese Numbers

| Numbers | Kanji (based on Chinese characters) | Romaji (in Roman alphabet) |
|---------|-------------------------------------|----------------------------|
| 1 | 一 | ichi |
| 2 | 二 | ni |
| 3 | 三 | san |
| 4 | 四 | shi, yon |
| 5 | 五 | go |
| 6 | 六 | roku |
| 7 | 七 | shichi, nana |
| 8 | 八 | hachi |
| 9 | 九 | kyū, kū |
| 10 | 十 | jū |

Practice counting to 10. Pronounce the numbers like this:
1 [eechee]; 2 [nee]; 3 [sahn]; 4 [shee] or [yon]; 5 [go]; 6 [rokoo]; 7 [shee-chee] or [nahnah]; 8 [hahchee]; 9 [kyoo] or [koo]; 10 [joo].

## Activity 3

Copy the letters from the box below on a sheet of paper. Try to find all the Japanese numbers from 1 to 10 written in romaji. The first one has been done for you. (The forms *yon, nana,* and *kyu* are not included.)

| k | o | k | u | h | n | i | r | i | i |
|---|---|---|---|---|---|---|---|---|---|
| j | u | k | i | s | a | n | e | h | o |
| r | o | u | g | c | h | c | c | s | h |
| r | h | s | o | i | c | i | h | a | c |
| o | s | h | s | h | i | c | h | i | i |

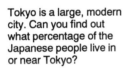

Tokyo is a large, modern city. Can you find out what percentage of the Japanese people live in or near Tokyo?

*Courtesy of the Japan National Tourist Organization*

# Japanese Words You Know

Do you recognize any of these words? Say the words to yourself. Do they sound familiar?

bata                    hamu                    sarada

Japanese has borrowed many words from English. During the American occupation after World War II, many English words were added to the Japanese vocabulary. The spelling of the borrowed words represents the way the Japanese pronounce them. For example, the letter *l* becomes an *r* sound in Japanese pronunciation.

## Activity 4

**Match the Japanese (romaji) words in the left column with the English words on the right.**

| *Japanese (Romaji)* | *English* |
|---|---|
| 1. bata | dessert |
| 2. supu | bacon |
| 3. choppu | sauce |
| 4. hamu | salad |
| 5. beikon | soup |
| 6. sosu | butter |
| 7. sarada | ham |
| 8. chīzu | cheese |
| 9. remon | chop |
| 10. dezato | coffee |
| 11. naifu | knife |
| 12. kōhī | lemon |

---

**Bonus Question**

What is *rajio? tepurekoda? tepu? fuirumu?*

## Greeting People

Japanese people bow their heads slightly when greeting someone rather than shaking hands.

The expressions for greeting people are printed below, in *romaji*. Read them and check the helpful hints on pronunciation.

| *Japanese* | *Meaning* |
|---|---|
| Konnichi wa. | Hello. (used from about 10:00 A.M. until late afternoon) |
| Ogenki desu ka. | How are you? |
| Genki desu. | Fine. |
| Hajimemashite dōzo yoroshiku. | How do you do? Pleased to meet you. |
| Arigatō. | Thank you. |
| Sayōnara. | Good-bye. |

### Helpful Hints on Pronunciation:

[koneechee wa]
[ogenkee des ka] (*g* as in *go*)
[genkee des]
[hajeemaymashtay dohzo yoroshkoo]
[areegatoh]
[sayohnara]

Suppose your class took a trip to the United Nations Building in New York City, and a group of Japanese students was also visiting. Using the expressions you just learned, show how you would greet one another.

## Japanese Foods

In a traditional Japanese home, you would sit on a *tatami* to eat. A *tatami* is a straw mat used to cover the floor. You would have removed your shoes at the door. You would enjoy your meal using chopsticks. Today, many Japanese homes also have Western-style tables and chairs, and for some types of food, knives and forks may be used.

Many Japanese restaurants have a tatami Japanese-style room and a Western-style room. In the Western-style room, customers sit at tables or at the *sushi* bar. They may eat with either forks or chopsticks.

Here are the names of a few Japanese foods. See if you can identify them before checking the answers below.

1. Sushi
2. Sukiyaki
3. Sashimi

4. Tempura
5. Teriyaki
6. Maki-zushi

## Beverages

Tea is an important part of Japanese culture. The Japanese people also drink milk, coffee, juice, and various soft drinks.

## How Is It Made?

Look back at the numbered list of Japanese foods. Which ones did you identify correctly?

1. Mound of cold rice, usually topped with or wrapped in raw fish, seaweed, or vegetables
2. Mixture of thin beef slices and vegetables cooked in soy sauce
3. Bite-sized pieces of raw seafood of different varieties
4. Fish and/or vegetables dipped in batter and deep-fried (*tempura* means "deep-fried")
5. Fish or meat broiled with soy sauce and sake [*sah-kee*], a wine made from rice.
6. Rice wrapped in seaweed, usually with fish and vegetables

For dessert, Japanese people like to eat fruit or small cakes or sweets.

---

## Activity 5

Create a Japanese lunch menu for your classmates. Write out what will be served. Design the menu with an authentic Japanese block print, a photo, or a drawing. You can use resources in your school library—an encyclopedia, books about Japan, *National Geographic* magazine.

Many Japanese dishes use fish and even seaweed.

*Courtesy of the Japan National Tourist Organization*

## Try a Japanese Recipe

Here is a recipe you might wish to try. Work with an adult member of your family to prepare the food.

---

**Recipe to Try**

### Asparagus Tempura

*Ingredients*

2 cups ice water
$1^2/_3$ cups all-purpose flour
1 egg yolk
$1/_8$ teaspoon baking soda

3 cups vegetable oil
2 pounds thin raw asparagus,
  trimmed
salt to taste

*Instructions*

Combine the first four ingredients in a medium mixing bowl and beat until smooth. Cover and refrigerate until ready to use.

To prepare, heat the oil in a shallow pan to 375°F. Dip asparagus in the batter and fry in batches until golden brown. Drain on paper towels, salt lightly, and serve immediately.

## A Japanese Song

To think of Japan is to think of cherry blossoms. From late March to early May in different parts of the country, "Hana-mi," cherry-blossom viewing, is a favorite pastime. Many people enjoy picnics, "sakura parties," singing and dancing under these lovely blossoms.

# Cherry Blossoms
### *Sakura*

Sakura, Sakura, lovely flowers filling the trees, clouds of blossoms sway in the breeze, scented petals gently come down.
Tell of springtime all through the town.
Sakura, Sakura, we see cherry trees bloom.

*Courtesy of Montgomery County, Maryland, Public Schools*

## Topics for Discussion and Review

1. How has Japan changed since the end of World War II (1945)?
2. Name some of the main products exported by Japan.
3. Name two effects China had on the Japanese language.
4. Explain the Japanese attitude toward their traditions. How is it similar to our attitude? How is it different?

## Activities and Projects

1. Below is a list of topics related to Japanese culture. Choose *five* to investigate. Write a short report and be prepared to discuss *two* of them with the class.

   | | |
   |---|---|
   | calligraphy | karate/judo |
   | castles in Japan | kendō |
   | fans | kimono |
   | festivals in Japan | kokeshi dolls |
   | foods of Japan | origami |
   | Japanese gardens | samurai |
   | Japanese history | sumō |
   | Kabuki theater | tea ceremony |

2. Tell why Hiroshima and Nagasaki are special cities in the world. Prepare a set of questions for your class on what happened in those cities in August 1945.
3. Prepare a report on the martial arts. Include pictures. Try to interview someone who has earned a black belt.
4. Describe the Cherry Blossom Festival held in Washington, D.C., each spring. Explain the history and tradition of these cherry trees and their connection to Japan.

---

### Mystery Words

The mystery words are all Japanese words used in English. Look up the meaning of the words below in a dictionary.

futon        hibachi        karate        tofu

# CHAPTER ELEVEN

# EXPLORING CHINESE,
## CHINA, AND ITS PEOPLE

你好

## Welcome to China

"Within the four seas, all are brothers," Confucius once said. Could it be that this wise and highly revered philosopher* might have had the international language problem in mind when he uttered these words?

Can you estimate how many people speak Chinese? China is one of the world's largest countries in area, and it has more people than any other country. In fact, it has over a billion people!

---

*Use a dictionary to find out the meaning of this word. What language does it come from?

# Map of China

## Activity 1

A.   Do some research. Find out which are the world's largest countries in area.

B.   Study the map of China.

      1.   What countries are China's neighbors?

      2.   What great river flows through China?

The Great Wall of China.
Find out when it was
built and why.

*Courtesy of Diana K. Brosnan*

# China's Historical Highlights

China is one of the oldest countries in the world. It is almost five thousand years old. (Just to compare: Our country is barely over two hundred years old! When Columbus set out to find a new route to the East in 1492, China already had a long history!)

China was ruled by emperors in its early history. The period of time covering the rule of one family or group is called a *dynasty*. Each dynasty in China's history had its own name. Emperors ruled China until 1912.

During Europe's Middle Ages, China was the world's most advanced country. It had a written language, an organized government, dikes and canals, agriculture, refined handicrafts, a silk industry, pottery and porcelain, the abacus, and the technology to make explosives.

## Activity 2

**A.** **Here are the names of three Chinese dynasties. Find out the dates each dynasty began and ended.**

*Qin* dynasty            *Song* dynasty            *Ming* dynasty

(You may find the Qin and Song dynasties listed under *Ch'in* and *Sung*. This is because there is more than one way to write Chinese words in the Roman alphabet. You will learn about the most commonly used system in this chapter.)

**B.** **During the Song dynasty, a famous traveler from Italy visited China. Can you name this man? What interesting things did he take back to Italy?**

These warriors date from the Qin dynasty, about 200 B.C. Over 7,000 such figures were found in a tomb, lined up as if ready for battle. They are made of terra cotta (a baked clay).

*Courtesy of the China National Tourist Office*

## China after 1912

- After the last dynasty was overthrown in 1912, China became a republic. It tried to establish a democratic form of government.
- Sun Yat-sen was China's first leader during this period. He died in 1925. Later, General Chiang Kai-shek came to power. Both men worked to help China become a unified country.
- During the 1930s and 1940s, there was a long civil war between the Nationalists under Chiang, who wanted China to be democratic, and the Communists. The country was also at war with Japan over territory that Japan had seized.
- In 1949, Chiang was defeated by the Communists led by Mao Zedong. The Nationalists then set up a government on the island of Taiwan. Find Taiwan on the map. It is near China. This government was called the Republic of China. Chiang Kai-shek was its president. It represented China in the United Nations until 1971.
- Mao Zedong controlled the government of mainland China from 1949 until his death in 1976. Mainland China had a Communist government under Mao.
- In 1976 Mao Zedong died. The leaders who have followed him have also been Communist.
- The People's Republic of China is a member of the United Nations. It replaced Nationalist China in 1971.
- In 1979, our government established official relations with the People's Republic of China. This means that our country trades with China and exchanges students and teachers, as well as ambassadors and other government officials.

## China Today

Today the capital of China is Beijing [bay**jing**]. It used to be pronounced Peking [pee**king**]. There is a central Communist government that administers laws to the provinces. There are other regions, cities, and counties that elect their own representatives. The head of state is called the chairman instead of the president.

Some Chinese would like to have a more democratic country. In 1989, thousands of students took part in large demonstrations for freedom in Tian'anmen Square in Beijing. The government violently put down the students' movement.

Tian'anmen Square and
the Monument of People's
Heroes

*Courtesy of Diana K. Brosnan*

## The Chinese People

The family has always been important to the Chinese people. Extended families, including grandparents and other close relatives, often live in the same home. The children greatly respect the elders in the family.

The Chinese also feel connected in a spiritual way to their ancestors and have great respect for them.

Because there are so many people in China (remember, at least a billion), the Chinese people are used to living and working in crowded conditions.

The Chinese may have many traditions because they represent the oldest continuing civilization in the world—almost five thousand years!

---

### Activity 3

On a sheet of paper, copy each name from the list below. Find interesting information about each place, and then write a brief paragraph about it. You may want to prepare a travel brochure for one of the places.

> Beijing
> Guilin
> Hong Kong
> Imperial Palace
> Shanghai
> the Great Wall
> Xi'an
> Tian'anmen

## Chinese Festivals and Holidays

One of the most exciting traditions is the Chinese New Year. This is a family celebration. It takes place in late January or early February. It is sometimes called the *lunar new year* because it comes after the new moon. (You may know that *luna* is the Latin word for "moon.")

Would you like to be at a Chinese New Year's celebration? It usually lasts for four days! There is much feasting, exchanging of gifts, a parade of good-luck dragons, fireworks, and music. Red is the main color used for New Year's decorations.

These celebrations also take place in the United States in cities that have a Chinese-American population.

Other Chinese holidays that are based on the lunar calendar are the Dragon Festival at the end of May and the Autumn Moon Festival. People gather to look at the full moon and to eat moon-shaped cakes.

Here are some other holidays celebrated in China: May 4 (Youth Day); October 1 and 2, called the National Holiday, marking the official beginning of the Communist government in 1949.

## Let's Explore the Chinese Language

In this book, you are learning about different alphabets, such as the Greek, Roman, and so on. Does every language have an alphabet? Discuss this question with a classmate. (Do not read ahead. Discuss the question based on the knowledge you already have.)

Chinese is one of the world's languages that do not use an alphabet. Many Chinese characters are based on pictographs and ideographs, meaning characters based on pictures. The Chinese system has been in use for thirty-five centuries!

Remember language families from chapter 4? The language family to which Chinese belongs is called the Sino-Tibetan* family of languages.

---

*Check an unabridged dictionary or an encyclopedia for a listing of the Sino-Tibetan family, which includes the languages of Burma and Thailand.

## Some Interesting Language Facts

- The different "dialects"* of China not only *sound* different, they have different vocabularies and even grammars.
- The Chinese have adopted the Northern Mandarin dialect as the official language of the country. Approximately 885 million people speak this dialect. It is taught in the schools.
- Other major dialects spoken in different areas are Cantonese, Wu, and Southern Min.

Even though the Chinese have many spoken dialects, the written language is basically the same everywhere. In the 1950s, the Chinese government adopted a system called *pinyin*. It really means "spell sound." The pinyin system was not intended to replace the Chinese characters, but to serve as a pronunciation aid. Chinese schoolchildren learn the pinyin system in first grade to help them begin to read. Pinyin uses the Roman alphabet.

---

**Mystery Word**

ROMANIZATION

Can you guess what it means?
*Your clue: roman*
It means: Writing the sounds in the _____ alphabet.

---

In Mandarin Chinese, the pronunciation uses four basic tones. *Tone* is the pitch of your voice in saying a word. The four tones in Mandarin Chinese are:

| ─ | ╱ | ⌣ | ╲ |
|---|---|---|---|
| 1st tone high and even | 2nd tone low rising to high | 3rd tone lower than the second tone; rising as in a question | 4th tone high falling toward low |

It is important to use the correct tone when saying a Chinese word since two words can have the same sound but different tones and different meanings.

---

*A dialect is a variation of a language.

## Activity 4

Pronounce the English word *knee*, using the four tones on the preceding page.

---

### Learn to Recognize

Can you recognize the symbols of the tones?

| *Chinese* | *How It Sounds* | *Meaning* |
|---|---|---|
| 謝謝你 | [shièh-shieh nĕe] | Thank you |

The Ch'ang Chiang (Yangtze) River is China's largest river, 3,434 miles long. It flows through some of China's richest agricultural land. In this picture, it is passing through a picturesque gorge.

*Courtesy of the China National Tourist Office*

## About Chinese Characters

- The modern system of Chinese characters developed from *pictographs* (symbols representing the object) and, later, *ideographs* (symbols representing an idea).
- There are approximately 50,000 Chinese characters.
- The average Chinese person knows between 3,000 and 5,000 characters.
- You need to know about 3,000 characters to read an average Chinese newspaper.

- For centuries, Chinese characters were written in columns and read from top to bottom, right to left. Today the characters are sometimes written in the same manner as English, from left to right. A newspaper might have some articles printed in the "old" style and some in the "new" style.
- Some Chinese people might not understand one another's dialects, but they can communicate by *writing out* their sentences. Each person could read the characters according to his or her own dialect. So the written characters can serve as a kind of common Chinese language all over the country.

## Activity 5

**A.  Let's pronounce and read the pinyin for the written Chinese below. Do not forget the correct tone!**

| Meaning | Chinese Character | How It Sounds | Pinyin |
|---------|-------------------|---------------|--------|
| Good morning | 你早 | [nee dzow] | nǐ zǎo |

Practice saying the greeting with a partner. Teach a member of your family to say it. Practice greeting each other at home.

**B.   Writing Chinese**

person

mountain

rain

sun

Try to draw the characters above in slow motion on your paper. The arrows will tell you which way to make your strokes. Use a medium-point marker. Follow the numbers. Remember, great care and pride are virtues of Chinese penmanship.

## Some Greetings

If you were to visit Chinatown in San Francisco, New York, Chicago, or Washington, D.C., or the China Pavilion at Disney World, how would you greet someone politely in Chinese?

| Chinese Characters | How It Sounds | Pinyin | Meaning |
|---|---|---|---|
| 你早 | [nee dzow] | nǐ zǎo | Good morning (till 10:00 A.M.) |
| 你好 | [nee how] (h like Bach) | nǐ hǎo | Good afternoon/ Good evening/Hello (anytime) |
| 晚安 | [wahn ahn] | wǎn-ǎn | Good night |
| 再見 | [dzai gee-en] | zài jiàn | Good-bye |

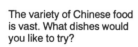

### Activity 6

Practice the greetings above with a classmate. Look at the "How It Sounds" column for the pronunciation and the "Pinyin" column for the tone marks. Check back on page 165 for help with the tones. Look carefully at the characters. Do you notice any that are similar?

The variety of Chinese food is vast. What dishes would you like to try?

*Courtesy of Diana K. Brosnan*

# Chinese Cooking

Chinese cooking is known for its mixture of rice, noodles, vegetables, and meats. Chinese food varies from region to region. Chinese cooking is popular all over the United States.

Sichuan (often spelled Szechuan) and Hunan dishes are spiced with red peppers, ginger, and garlic. They represent the Western Chinese style of cooking.

Eastern Chinese dishes are based on recipes from the Shanghai region. These dishes often use vinegar, sugar, and soy sauce as ingredients in flavoring the food. You may have heard the term *sweet and sour* used to describe this type of cooking.

Northern Chinese cuisine uses more wheat, noodles, and dumplings than rice. Lamb, beef, duck, sesame oil, and garlic are all part of this cuisine.

Southern Chinese cuisine uses many fresh vegetables in the preparation of dishes. A well-known ingredient is the water chestnut. Chicken, roast duck, and pork are favorite meats.

Tea is a favorite beverage all over China.

# Topics for Discussion and Review

1. How would you describe the Chinese language to someone who didn't know anything about it? How old is it?
2. Explain the difference between the *Republic of China* and the *People's Republic of China*.
3. Find out why the official language of China was designated as Mandarin. Who were the mandarins?
4. Find out the origin and meaning of these Chinese words used in English: *chow mein, kowtow, sampan, shantung*.

---

### Mystery Words

What are they?

- Pekingese
- Chow Chow

## Activities and Projects

1.  Visit your library and learn more about China. Some interesting topics are:

    | | |
    |---|---|
    | pandas | the last emperor of China: |
    | Chinese cooking | Pu Yi |
    | Singapore | Chinese tea |
    | Taiwan | "The Forbidden City" |
    | Chinese writing (calligraphy) | the Chinese New Year |
    | silk and the silkworm | Chinese folk sports |
    | the Ming dynasty | the Great Wall of China |
    | the Manchu (or Ch'ing) | Temple of Heaven monument |
    | dynasty | Confucius |

    Choose *five* of the above topics. Prepare a "fact sheet" about each chosen topic. After your teacher has checked them, choose one sheet for your teacher to distribute to your class.

2.  Look up *Marco Polo* in an encyclopedia or a biographical dictionary. When did he arrive in China? What did he find?

3.  Have you ever used an abacus in math class? Find out what it is and how it is used.

# CHAPTER TWELVE

# EXPLORING ARABIC
## AND THE ARABIC-SPEAKING WORLD

أهـلا و سـهلا

---

*How It Sounds*
[ah**lan** wa-sah**lan**]

*Arabic Writing*
أهـلا و سـهلا
(Read from right to left)

*Meaning*
Welcome!

---

Arabic is the official language of twenty-one countries in the Middle East and North Africa, spoken by about 185 million people. Look at the map. What do you know about these countries? Have any of them been in the newspapers lately? Listen for news about these countries on television.

# The Arabic-Speaking World

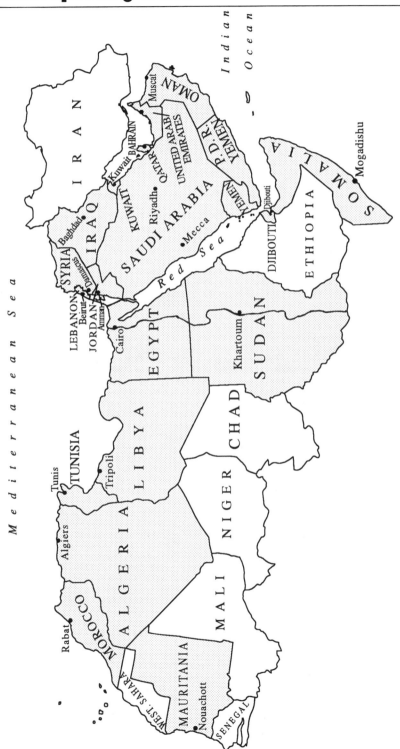

## Activity 1

**A.** **On a sheet of paper, copy the name of each country shown on the map. (Do not write in this book.) Fill in the blank letters as you write the name of the country.**

A _ g e r _ a                           O _ _ n
B a h r _ _ _                           Q _ t _ r
D _ i b _ _ t i                         S _ _ d i  A _ a b i a
E _ _ _ _                               S o _ a l _ a
I _ _ q                                 S u _ _ _
J o _ d a n                             S _ r i a
K u _ a i t                             T _ _ i s i a
L _ b _ _ o n                           U n i t e d  A _ a b
L i _ y _                                 E m i _ _ t e s*
M a u _ i _ _ n i a                     Y _ m _ n  A r _ b
M o _ o c _ o                            R _ _ u b l _ _

Are there other countries where Arabic is spoken? Check in the encyclopedia.

There is one country in the Middle East where Arabic is one of two official languages. Do you know the country? Here's a hint: Look at one of the chapters of this book.

This picture shows the rooftops of Cairo. It is the capital of which country?

*Courtesy of I. Yehiel*

---

*Word research:* Emir [emeer] and Sheik [shake]
*Clues:* Emir—emirate; Sheik—sheikdom. Be prepared to tell the class what the two words mean.

B.   Choose an Arabic-speaking country of interest to you. Prepare a short report for the class telling about: its location, its capital, different kinds of clothing, its interesting customs, and its people.

## Arabic's Word Gifts to English!

Did you know that we have English words that came from Arabic? You'll learn about some of them in this activity.

---

### Activity 2

**Meaning Match**

Read each definition. On a sheet of paper, write the English word that matches it. You will find the English words on page 182 in this chapter. They are all from Arabic.

1.   A substance that is useful in industry, but is harmful to the body
2.   A branch of mathematics; you study it in middle and high school!
3.   The highest ranking officer in the navy
4.   In chemistry, it makes acid neutral
5.   Sky blue
6.   A Muslim house of worship
7.   A symbol meaning "empty," or "nothing"
8.   Imaginary creatures in Muslim legends
9.   Islamic name for God
10.  The highest point, the top, the point directly overhead
11.  Another name for *couch*
12.  A place for storing military weapons
13.  A frozen dessert made from fruit juice, water, and sugar
14.  A sweet, thick liquid used on pancakes and waffles
15.  Large stuffed mat used on a bed

## The Arabic Alphabet

In Arabic, one writes from right to left instead of from left to right. The first letter of the Arabic alphabet is *alef,* which corresponds to our *a*. The second letter of the alphabet is *beh*, which corresponds to our *b*. There are other letters that correspond to letters in our alphabet but they are not in the same order. For example, the letter *del* corresponds to our *d*, but it is the eighth letter instead of the fourth. The last letter of the Arabic alphabet is *yeh*. (Remember to read from right to left!)

⟵

| ا | ب | ت | ث | ج | ح | خ |
|---|---|---|---|---|---|---|
| alef | beh | teh | theh | jeem | heh* | kheh |

| د | ذ | ر | ز | س | ش | ص |
|---|---|---|---|---|---|---|
| del | thel | reh | zein | seen | sheen | sawd |

| ض | ط | ظ | ع | غ | ف | ق |
|---|---|---|---|---|---|---|
| dawd | tuh | zuh | ain | ghain | feh | kawf |

| ك | ل | م | ن | هـ | و | ي |
|---|---|---|---|---|---|---|
| calf | lam | meem | noon | heh* | waw | yeh |

As you read the words above that are written in Roman letters under the Arabic, keep in mind that these words are the *names* of the letters, not the *sounds* of the letters.

Show the Arabic alphabet to a friend. Try to recite it together, using the names of the letters.

# Interesting Facts about Arabic

## Language Facts

- There are twenty-six letters in the Roman alphabet and twenty-eight in the Arabic alphabet.
- Of all the different alphabets in the world, the Arabic alphabet is the second most widely used. Which alphabet is *most* widely used? The Roman or Latin alphabet, the one you are now reading.

---

*Both of these letters represent a sound like *h*. The "heh" sound in the first row is a heavier *h* as in *hoot*, with a roughness in the throat. The "heh" sound in the last row is a lighter *h* as in *hear.*

- Do you know the word for the fine art of beautiful handwriting? It is called *calligraphy.** Like the Chinese and the Japanese, Arabic-speaking people are proud of their calligraphy. They use it for decoration as well as communication.
- The Arabs also use a style of ornamentation with wavy or curved lines that looks like Arabic script. This style is called *arabesque* [ara**besk**]. Sometimes Arabic script is added to the design.

The beautiful patterns of Arabic calligraphy are true works of art.

*Courtesy of Clarence Wachner*

- We have noted that there are twenty-eight letters in the Arabic alphabet. There are twenty-five consonants and three vowels. The vowels are *alef* : 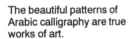 *waw* : و and *yeh* : ي . Several symbols are used above or below the letters to show changes in the uses of words in the sentence.
- Surprise! There are no Arabic capital letters.
  You have already learned that Arabic words are written from right to left. What other language do you know about that is written from right to left?

## Family History of Arabic

1. Arabic belongs to the Semitic language family, like Hebrew.
2. Arabic began about 600 B.C. Its writing system is descended from Egyptian hieroglyphics. Our alphabet is descended from this writing system, too.

---

*Find out from which language the word originated. What does the suffix *-graph* mean? In which chapter of this book would you find it talked about?

### Arab Connections with the European World

1. About A.D. 700, Arabic-speaking Moors from North Africa conquered Spain. They occupied Spain until 1492.
2. In the eleventh and twelfth centuries, European kings sent large armies to recapture places in the Holy Land, or Palestine, that the Christians considered sacred. These places had been under Arab rule for about six hundred years. The expeditions are very famous in history. What were they called?*
3. Look up *Arabs* and *Moors* in the encyclopedia. You will find that the Moors were Arabic-speaking Muslims who invaded and ruled Spain for hundreds of years. Draw a conclusion about the number of years Arabic-speaking cultures greatly influenced Spain and other parts of Europe.
4. The Arab world had many scholars. People from all over Europe went to study medicine, chemistry, and astronomy with the Moors in Spain and other Arab centers of learning.
5. Some Arabic words entered Spanish and other languages.

# Greetings in Arabic

Try speaking in Arabic. Pronounce the "How It Sounds" column, and then look at the Arabic. Don't forget to look at the Arabic from right to left.

|   | *Arabic* | *How It Sounds* | *Meaning* |
|---|---|---|---|
| 1. | السلام عليكم | [as-sa**laam** a**lay**kom] | Hello! |
| 2. | و عليكم السلام | [wa a**lay**kom as salaam] | Hello! (reply) |
| 3. | كيف حالك؟ | [keef **ha**lak] | How are you? |
| 4. | بخير | [bikhayr] | Fine! |
| 5. | و انت؟ | [wa-**an**ta] | And you? |

---

*The word for these expeditions comes from a Latin word: *crux.* Find out what it means. What does *crux* mean in English?

| | *Arabic* | *How It Sounds* | *Meaning* |
|---|---|---|---|
| 6. | بخير | [bikh**ayr**] | Fine! |
| 7. | مع السلامة | [maa al sa**laam**a] | Good-bye! |
| | نعم | [**na**am] | yes |
| | لا | [la] | no |
| | شكرا | [**shook**ran] | thank you |

### Notes:

- Arabic words are often pronounced in various ways in different Arab countries, but they are always written the same.
- Do you know a Hebrew word that reminds you of *Salaam?* *As-salaam alaykom* means "Peace be unto you." The Hebrew word also means "peace."

## Let's Count in Arabic

| *Arabic Numbers as Used Today* | *Arabic Symbol* | *Arabic Name* | *How It Sounds* |
|---|---|---|---|
| 0 | • | صفر | [sifr] (*i* as in *sit*) |
| 1 | ١ | واحد | [**wah**ed] (*e* as in *bed*) |
| 2 | ٢ | اثنان | [**eth**nan] (*a* as in *cake*) |
| 3 | ٣ | ثلاثة | [tha**lath**ah] |
| 4 | ٤ | اربعة | [**ar**baa] |
| 5 | ٥ | خمسة | [**kha**msah] |
| 6 | ٦ | ستة | [**sit**tah] |
| 7 | ٧ | سبعة | [**sab**aa] |
| 8 | ٨ | ثمانية | [tham**an**ya] |
| 9 | ٩ | تسعة | [**tis**ah] (*i* as in *sit*) |
| 10 | ١• | عشرة | [**ash**ara] |

Remember that Arabic words are read from right to left.

---

**Activity 3**

A. **Practice saying the greetings in Arabic with a partner.**

B. **Count from 0 to 10 in Arabic. Then count from 10 to 0.**

## Arabic Numbers

The numbers we use every day came from the Arabs. We even *call* them Arabic numbers.

The number system the Arabs borrowed from India had nine symbols and a dot. The Arabs used this dot as a zero, or cipher. (Look back at the list of Arabic numbers. Notice the word for the *dot: sifr.* It reminds us of *cipher.*) The dot became a circle—*0*.

In this box, we trace the development of the word for *zero* according to the opinion of some scholars.

---

### Word Detectives

#### FOLLOW THIS TRAIL:

| *Hindu* | | *Arabic* | | *Latin* | | *Italian* | | *English* |
|---------|---|----------|---|---------|---|-----------|---|-----------|
| sunya | → | sifr | → | ziphirum | → | zero | → | zero |

---

Some scientists who have studied the history of mathematics believe that the Hindus had the concept of "the empty place" but they did not have a name for it.

When writing numbers consecutively across a page, Arabic-speaking people write them from right to left.

◄————————————————

10, 9, 8, 7, 6, 5, 4, 3, 2, 1, 0

But two or more digits, such as 76, 350, 4780, are combined in the same way we do. All mathematical operations are carried out in the same manner as everywhere else in the world.

# Famous Writings in Arabic

### The Qur'an

The main religion of the Arab world is called Islam. People who follow this religion are called Muslims. It was established about A.D. 615 by the religious leader called the Prophet Muhammad.

Muhammad's words were written in the Arabic language in a book called the *Qur'an*. Have you seen the word *Koran?* This is the common English way of writing this word. The *Qur'an* helped to spread the Arabic language as more people were converted to Islam in the Middle East and other areas.

The Islamic religion is central to the history of the Arabic-speaking world. This is a picture of a mosque in Saudi Arabia, the home of some of the most sacred sites in Islam.

*Courtesy of the Kingdom of Saudi Arabia, Ministry of Information*

### Arab Folktales

Have you ever read the stories of *Aladdin and His Magic Lamp, Ali Baba and the Forty Thieves,* or *Sinbad the Sailor?* You may have seen film and cartoon versions of these stories.

Did you know that these stories are part of a collection of Arabic folktales and poems handed down from generation to generation?

Ask your friends if they've heard of a woman named Scheherazade [shahhairuh**zahd**].

If you look up her name in the encyclopedia or in the library file, you will probably be referred to the title *Arabian Nights* or *Thousand and One Nights.* This is the title of the collection of Arabic folktales mentioned above.

Of course, there are many modern Arab writers. Some live in the United States.

## Arab Foods

Check your neighborhood supermarket.

- Look for "pocket bread." The word you will see in the supermarket for pocket bread is **pita.** Bring a sample of pita bread to class. Show the "pocket," where you can put any kind of food you like for a meal. Do you think this idea is better than the idea of a sandwich?
- Have you ever watched **shish kebab** being prepared? (They are pieces of lamb with onions and tomatoes grilled on a skewer.)
- **Baklawa** [bahk**lah**wah] is a well-known dessert. It is made of thin layers of pastry filled with nuts—almonds and pistachios—steeped in honey.

A rich variety of foods makes up Middle Eastern cuisine. Vegetables and fruits are very popular; some foods are cooked wrapped in grape leaves.

The Islamic religion forbids the eating of pork. Lamb, fish, beef, and poultry are common in Arab dishes. Pigeon is also served. (Have you ever eaten Cornish hen? Could pigeon be considered in the same category?)

Foods such as hamburgers and the American version of pizza are also becoming popular in parts of the Arab world.

## Activity 4

### A.   Some Famous Places

Choose a place name from the right-hand column and match it to the correct
description in the left-hand column. Look at the map on page 172. Write your
answers on a sheet of paper.

| | |
|---|---|
| 1. The capital of Egypt | a. Nile |
| 2. Capital of an oil-rich country of the same name | b. Cairo |
| 3. Capital of Syria—mentioned in the New Testament | c. The Great Sphinx |
| | d. Beirut |
| 4. The most important city of Islam | e. Baghdad |
| 5. Former capital of the Muslim Empire, in Iraq | f. Kuwait |
| 6. A famous monument near Egyptian pyramids (head of a person and body of a lion) | g. Damascus |
| | h. Mecca |
| 7. Once-beautiful capital of Lebanon now ravaged by civil war | |
| 8. A long African river, scene of early civilization | |

### B.   More about Arabic Words: Answers to Activity 2

Here are the answers to Activity 2 on page 174.

| | |
|---|---|
| 1. alcohol | 9. Allah |
| 2. algebra | 10. zenith |
| 3. admiral | 11. sofa |
| 4. alkali | 12. arsenal |
| 5. azure | 13. sherbet |
| 6. mosque | 14. syrup |
| 7. cipher | 15. mattress |
| 8. jinni (or djinni) | |

Write a composition or sketch, using at least four of the above
words. Work with your class, partner, or group. Your sketch can be
funny, mysterious, sad, or happy!

**Example:** The sun was at its *zenith* and the town clock was striking
twelve. It was Saturday and Michael was still lying on the *sofa* trying
to wake up. He realized he did not have his *algebra* homework for
Monday. He thought, "I wish a *jinni* would appear and do my
homework!"

---

### Bonus Word

*Explain this statement:* Paris is the *mecca* of fashion designers.

---

## Topics for Discussion and Review

1. Describe the Arab influence on the Western world.
2. Explain the importance of the *zero* concept. Suppose you were suddenly transported to ancient Rome. How would you explain the use of zero and Arabic numerals to a group of students?
3. Tell what you have learned about the Arabic language.
4. List the Arabic-speaking countries. Name some of the most famous places in these countries.

## Activities and Projects

1. Find a copy of *Arabian Nights* in the library and bring it to class. Be prepared to tell or read one of the stories to the class, using dramatic effects.
2. Investigate the Crusades. Prepare a report showing how these expeditions affected the education and culture of Western Europe.
3. If you know an Arabic-speaking person, interview him or her and report back to the class. If possible, arrange with your teacher to invite the person to class. A few questions you might ask during the interview:

   - What Arab country are you from?
   - How long have you been in the U.S.? (Perhaps the person was born here of Arab parents.)
   - What are some of the interesting places in your country?

4. Do a special study of the camel. What is its history? To what animals is it related? How is it used in the desert?

## Mystery Words

MOGUL          NADIR          ALFALFA          MINARET

Find out what they mean. Write sentences using them.

# CHAPTER THIRTEEN

# EXPLORING THE HEBREW LANGUAGE,
## ISRAEL, AND ITS PEOPLE

שָׁלוֹם

## Who Speaks Hebrew?

Hebrew is an ancient and modern language.

You may have several classmates or friends who take Hebrew lessons after school. They may be Jewish. You can find out something about the Hebrew language by asking your Jewish friends or classmates who are studying it.

What are some other sources of information about Hebrew? If there is a synagogue* in your community, you could ask for information there. The Jewish people in many lands study Hebrew for religious reasons.

Your school library probably has books on the Hebrew language and the main country in which it is spoken.

---

*A *synagogue* is a Jewish place of worship. The person in charge of a synagogue is a *rabbi*.

Here are some questions to guide your investigation.

1. In what country is Hebrew an official language?
2. Where is that country located?
3. Where and why was that country established?
4. Why is it called "an old new land"?
5. That area is also called the Holy Land. Determine the reason for this name.
6. What world-famous book was originally written in the Hebrew language?
7. What is the Holy City? Why is it called that?

The city of Jerusalem is the site of many famous monuments. What do you know about the city?

*Courtesy of Ira Weiss*

## The Hebrew Language

Here is an important Hebrew word you can learn to say. This is how it sounds:

**Sha**l**om**

It means "peace." It is used as a greeting for both "hello" and "good-bye." In Hebrew, it looks like this:

שלום

Here are some important facts about this language:

• The Hebrew language is written from right to left.

- The Hebrew alphabet has no vowels. But the spoken language does have vowel *sounds*.
- To help beginners with pronunciation, dots and lines are used with the letters to show the vowel sounds.
- The alphabet in Hebrew is called *aleph-bet. Aleph* is not a vowel in Hebrew; it is a silent consonant, but it can function as a vowel sound in words that have a vowel sign.
- The Hebrew alphabet has twenty-two consonants.
- The Hebrew alphabet is related to the Greek alphabet and other alphabets of neighboring countries, such as Egypt.

**Example:**

| Greek | Hebrew |
|---|---|
| alpha | aleph |
| beta | bet |
| gamma (the third letter) | gimel (the third letter) |

## The Hebrew Alphabet

Here are the Hebrew alphabet characters listed in a column. The names of the characters have been written in the Roman alphabet to help you pronounce them.

### The Hebrew *Aleph-Bet*

| | Names | Sounds | | Names | Sounds |
|---|---|---|---|---|---|
| א | Aleph | Silent | ל | Lammed | l |
| ב, בּ | Bet, Vet | b, v | ם, מ | Mem | m |
| ג | Gimel | g as in *go* | ן, נ | Nun | n |
| ד | Dalet | d | ס | Samekh | s |
| ה | Heh | h | ע | Ayin | Silent |
| ו | Vav | v | ף, פ, פּ | Peh, Feh | p, f |
| ז | Zayin | z | ץ, צ | Tsade | ts as in *its* |
| ח | Khet | ch as in *Bach* | ק | Koph | k |
| ט | Tet | t | ר | Resh | r (trilled as in Spanish *burro*) |
| י | Yod | y as in *yell* | | | |
| ך, כ, כּ | Kaph, Khaph | k, kh | שׁ, שׂ | Shin, Sin | sh as in *show, s* |
| | | | ת, תּ | Tav | t |

**Activity 1**

**Recite the Hebrew alphabet, using words in the "Names" column.**

## Meeting New Friends

Now that you have been introduced to the Hebrew language, here is a skit for you and your classmates. Take turns acting it out!

As you look at each line of the Hebrew, what will you remember? Of course, look at each line from *right* to *left!*

| *Hebrew* | | *How It Sounds* | *Meaning* | |
|---|---|---|---|---|
| אילנה: שלום! | | [sha**lom**] | Ilana: | Hello! My |
| שמי אילנה. | | [shmee ee**lana**] | | name is Ilana. |
| מה שמך? | | [ma shim**kha**] | | What's your name? |
| דן: שמי דן. | | [shmee dahn. | Dan: | My name is |
| נעים מאד. | | na-**eem** mi-od] | | Dan. Pleased to meet you. |
| אילנה: יופי! | | [yofi!] | Ilana: | Wonderful! |
| להתראות! | | [li-**hitra**-ot] | | See you again! |

---

### Activity 2

**Work with a small group of classmates. Look at the Hebrew lines in the skit. Compare them with the list of sounds. How many words can you identify? Keep in mind that each word is read from right to left!**

**For eager beavers:** How many Hebrew letters in the skit can you recognize from the alphabet listing? Give the name of each letter that you recognize.

### More Hebrew Words to Say

| *Hebrew* | *How It Sounds* | *Meaning* |
|---|---|---|
| כֵּן. | [ken] | yes |
| לֹא. | [lo] | no |
| תּוֹדָה. | [to**da**] | thank you |
| בְּבַקָשָׁה. | [bevaka**shah**] | you're welcome; please |

# Count in Hebrew from 0 to 10

Below are the numbers from 0 to 10 and how they sound in Hebrew.

As you read each of the names in the "How It Sounds" column, look at each Hebrew word. Remember to direct your eyes from right to left when looking at each Hebrew word.

| Hebrew | Numbers | How It Sounds |
|--------|---------|---------------|
| אפס | 0 | [**efes**] |
| אחת | 1 | [a**khat**] |
| שתיים | 2 | [**shta**yim] |
| שלוש | 3 | [sha**losh**] |
| ארבע | 4 | [ar**ba**] |
| חמש | 5 | [kha**mesh**] |
| שש | 6 | [shesh] |
| שבע | 7 | [**sheva**] |
| שמונה | 8 | [**shmo**neh] |
| תשע | 9 | [**tesha**] |
| אשר | 10 | [**eser**] |

Looking into the city of Jerusalem from the Jaffa Gate

*Courtesy of Dallas Kennedy*

# English Connections

### Names of Hebrew Origin

Do you know anyone named David, Joshua, Jonathan, Nathan, Jacob, Adam, Rachel, Mary, Rebecca, Sarah, or Ruth?

These are names of Hebrew origin. Look up as many as you can in the unabridged dictionary or a dictionary of names and find out what each one really means.

Have you found the origin of your own name? What language did it come from? What does it mean?

### Hebrew Words Used in English

| | |
|---|---|
| amen | (said after a prayer or wish) |
| shekel | (unit of money in Israel) |
| Shabbat | (Sabbath, day of rest in Jewish and some other religions) |
| sak | (sack) |
| kinamon | (cinnamon) |

The Dome of the Rock is in the old part of Jerusalem. Now a museum, it used to be a Muslim place of worship.

*Courtesy of Dallas Kennedy*

# Israel: What Did You Find Out?

By this time, you may know that Hebrew is one of the official languages of the country of Israel. Israel has two official languages; the second is Arabic. English is also spoken by many people in Israel. Here are some facts about Israel.

1. Israel is an ancient land, thousands of years old. It is located in the Middle East. Most of the land it now occupies used to be called Palestine, and it is known as the Holy Land. Three religions originated in the Middle East: Judaism (the Jewish faith), Islam (the Muslim faith), and Christianity. People of many nationalities live in Israel, in addition to Jews and Arabs.

2. Modern Israel became an independent country in 1948 after World War II. During World War II, six million Jews were killed in concentration camps by the Nazis. This great tragedy is known as the Holocaust. Others were imprisoned in work camps or death camps, but were not killed. After the war, many of these people moved to Israel in order to establish it as a homeland for Jewish people from all over the world. Today, new immigrants continue to arrive.

3. The Hebrew language is almost four thousand years old! The Jewish scriptures were written in Hebrew, and are used in both the Jewish and Christian religions. These scriptures are called the *Old Testament* by Christians.

4. Palestine and the land of Israel were governed by various powers during their thousands of years of history, including the ancient Romans and Great Britain. Jews have lived in this area for over three thousand years; the Arabs have lived there for centuries as well.

## Activity 3

**Work with a partner to use this information on Israel to prepare a set of questions to quiz your classmates. Write your questions on a sheet of paper.**

**Bonus Question:** One of these countries does not border on Israel: Lebanon, Egypt, Saudi Arabia, Syria, Jordan. Which is it? Look carefully at the map.

## A Special Place Found in Israel

The *kibbutz* [kee-**bootz**] is a cooperative settlement where members work and live together, and divide the profits equally.

Sometimes the children live in a children's house on the kibbutz, but they usually sleep in the same cottage as their parents.

If you wish to refer to more than one kibbutz, you should say *kibbutzim* [keebootz**eem**].

What can *you* add to this information?

# The Hebrew Calendar

The Hebrew calendar divides the year into twelve months according to the cycles of the moon. The Hebrew lunar calendar dates back to the time of the ancient Hebrews. Find out what the current year is in this calendar.

Both the old Hebrew and modern Western calendars are used in official documents and daily activities in Israel. The Muslim calendar is also used.

## Jewish Holidays

Two important Jewish holidays are *Rosh Hashanah* (New Year) and *Yom Kippur* (Day of Atonement). In the modern calendar, they fall around middle or late September. *Passover* is celebrated for a full week in March or April, and *Hanukkah* is celebrated for eight days in December.

## Activity 4

A.  With the help of an encyclopedia, make one correct statement about each Israeli city listed here, and ask a classmate to identify the city.

Beersheba          Haifa          Jerusalem          Tel Aviv

B.    **Finding Out about Famous Jewish Americans**

There are many famous Americans of Jewish descent, including scientists, political figures, songwriters, filmmakers, entertainers, and so on.

Do you recognize these names? Check the encyclopedia, and then write a statement about each person to present to the class.

Albert Einstein            Henry Kissinger
Golda Meir                 George Gershwin
Irving Berlin              Barbra Streisand

What names can you add to this list?

## A Hebrew Song

*English*
Shalom to our friends;
Shalom to our friends;
Shalom, Shalom.
We'll see you again;
We'll see you again;
Shalom, Shalom.

*Hebrew*

שָׁלוֹם חֲבֵרִים
לְהִתְרָאוֹת שָׁלוֹם

## Shalom Havayreem

*Anonymous*                                    *Jewish melody*

SHALOM Irregular

Sha - lom, ha-vay-reem; sha - lom, ha-vay-reem; sha - lom, sha -
*(Translation: Peace, Friends.)*

lom. Li - hit - ra - ot; li - hit - ra - ot; sha - lom, sha - lom.

## Topics for Discussion and Review

1.  Summarize for your classmates what you have learned about the Hebrew language.
2.  Why is Israel called the Holy Land? Give its geographic location.
3.  What have you learned about writing in Hebrew? Write a short paragraph.

## Activities and Projects

1.  Find out as much as you can about Albert Einstein's life. Prepare a short report explaining to a student outside your class how Einstein's work helps us to understand the universe.
2.  Prepare a picture encyclopedia showing Israeli history, products, famous cities, and people.
3.  Prepare an oral or written report on the Holocaust.
4.  Where in the United States are the towns of Carmel and Bethlehem? Check in an atlas and an encyclopedia. Tell a few interesting facts about each of the places. What places in Israel are they named after?

---

### Mystery Words and Language Connections

Explain each word:
1.  Yiddish: What does it mean?
2.  Chutzpah: Who has it?
3.  *Sábado* is the Spanish word for a certain day of the week. What Hebrew word is related to it and which day of the week is it?

---

### A Final Word

שלום

# CHAPTER FOURTEEN

# EXPLORING SWAHILI
## AND SWAHILI-SPEAKING AREAS

## Jambo!

### Where Is Swahili Spoken?

Swahili is spoken in countries in East and Central Africa. It is spoken in:

- Kenya
- Tanzania
- Uganda
- eastern part of Zaire

It is one of the languages spoken in:

- Burundi
- Congo Republic
- Malawi
- Mozambique
- Rwanda
- Zambia

# Map of Africa

The buildings in downtown
Nairobi, Kenya

*Courtesy of the Kenya
Tourist Office*

# Swahili and Other Languages of Africa

### Language Facts to Consider

- More than eight hundred languages are spoken on the continent of Africa! Most of the people speak or understand more than one language or dialect. (Remember that a dialect is a variation of a language.)
- Swahili is spoken by about fifty million people.
- Think about it! Even though there are many languages in African countries, these countries must adopt one language for official business and communication. Some of the countries use English and French, but Swahili is also becoming popular for this purpose.
- Some African countries were colonies of France, England, or Portugal in the past. In addition to the African languages, French is used in parts of West Africa. Portuguese is used in parts of East Africa, and English in several countries, including Kenya, Liberia, and South Africa.

### Swahili Facts

- Swahili is actually an Arabic word! It means "coasts." The Swahili language developed as Arab and European traders and settlers came to East Africa, including the island of Zanzibar. Its proper name is Ki-Swahili, meaning "the language of the coasts."
- Swahili has borrowed words from Arabic, Portuguese, German, English, and the languages of India. Swahili was originally written in Arabic letters! British missionaries introduced the Roman alphabet in the 1700s.
- Swahili belongs to the Bantu family of languages.

## Activity 1

A. Locate on a map of Africa each of the countries where Swahili is spoken. Write a question to ask your classmates about each of these countries.

B. Find out why French, English, and Portuguese are used as official languages in some African countries south of the Sahara desert. Which countries are these?

# Greetings in Swahili

Imagine that you are meeting a student from Tanzania who is going to attend your school for a semester. To make the visitor feel more at home, you have learned a few words in Swahili to exchange greetings.

|  | *Swahili* | *How It Sounds** | *What It Means* |
|---|---|---|---|
| You: | Jambo (or) Hujambo. | [**jahm**bo] [hoo**jahm**bo] | You: Hello. |
| Visitor: | Sijambo. | [see**jahm**bo] | Visitor: Hello (reply). |
| You: | Jina lako nani? | [**jee**nah **lah**ko **nah**ni] | You: What is your name? |
| Visitor: | Jina langu ni (name). | [**jee**nah **lahn**goo nee] (name) | Visitor: My name is _____. |
| You: | U hali gani? | [oo **hah**lee **gah**nee] | You: How are you? |
| Visitor: | Sijambo asante. | [see**jahm**bo ah**sahn**tay] | Visitor: Fine, thanks. |
| Both: | Kwa heri! | [kwah **hai**ree] | Both: Good-bye! |

*The stress in Swahili is almost always on the next-to-last syllable.

## Activity 2

A.   Practice the greetings with a friend or classmate. (It is considered proper in Kenya and Tanzania to shake hands when greeting someone.)

B.   Copy the three forms of the dialogue on a sheet of paper. Save it in your notebook.

This market is in Zaire. Find Zaire on a map of Africa.

*Courtesy of Jim Evans*

## Additional Expressions for Your Word Bank

| *Swahili* | *How It Sounds* | *Meaning* |
|-----------|-----------------|-----------|
| Bwana | [**bwah**nah] | Mr. |
| Bibi | [**bee**bee] | Mrs. |
| Binti | [**been**tee] | Miss |
| hapana | [hah**pah**nah] | no |
| ndiyo | [**ndee**yo] | yes |
| sikitu | [see**kee**too] | You're welcome. |

## Counting in Swahili from 0 to 10

Here are the numbers from 0 to 10 in Swahili, together with how you can pronounce them.

| Numbers | Swahili | How It Sounds |
|---|---|---|
| 0 | sifuri | [see**foo**ree] |
| 1 | moja | [**mo**jah] |
| 2 | mbili | [**mbee**lee] |
| 3 | tatu | [**tah**too] |
| 4 | nne | [nay] |
| 5 | tano | [**tah**no] |
| 6 | sita* | [**see**tah] |
| 7 | saba* | [**sah**bah] |
| 8 | nane | [**nah**nay] |
| 9 | tisa* | [**tee**sah] |
| 10 | kumi | [**koo**mee] |

---

### Two Special Words

- *Uhuru* is the Swahili word for "freedom."
- *Harambe!* is the Swahili word for "together" or "moving forward."

---

## More Swahili Facts

- There are twenty-four letters in the Swahili alphabet, which has no *q* or *x*.
- The letter *g* is always "hard," as in *give*.
- The *r* should be rolled, using the tip of the tongue as in Spanish.
- Notice the words that begin with *n* or *m* followed by a consonant, like *ndiyo* and *mbili*. The letters *n* and *m* are not always followed by consonants when they begin words.

---

*These words are from the same language as the greeting *Salaam!* Name that language.

- One of the features of Bantu languages is that *prefixes* are usually used instead of *endings* to make changes in the words.

**Example:**
*Singular to plural:*
*ki*tabu=book
*vi*tabu=books

## Activity 3

**Vocabulary Roundup**

Have you learned these words?

| | | |
|---|---|---|
| jambo | Binti | u hali gani? |
| hujambo | hapana | kwa heri |
| sijambo | sikitu | jina langu ni _____ |
| Bwana | uhuru | ndiyo |
| Bibi | harambe | asante |

Say the words and expressions above. Then tell what each one means.

## Africa's Gifts

Read about the continent of Africa in an encyclopedia and in books from your school or public library.

From this information you will learn that:

- Africa is the ancestral home of African Americans.
- Many civilizations developed there thousands of years ago.
- People in different parts of Africa invented tools, built cities, and created beautiful art forms such as masks. They created music, wood carvings, and bronze statues, even before writing was developed! They also developed forms of government.
- The Great Sahara Desert separates the Arab countries of northern Africa from the other countries on the continent. The area south of the Sahara is called Sub-Saharan Africa.
- Creative art of Africa had great influence on artists of the twentieth century, such as Picasso.
- The *zeze* [**zay**zay] is an African stringed instrument.

The woman is celebrating Kwanzaa, an African-American holiday based on traditional African harvest celebrations. The word *kwanzaa* comes from a Swahili phrase that means "first fruits." Find out more about Kwanzaa.

*Courtesy of Harold Dorwin, Anacostia Museum, Washington, D.C.*

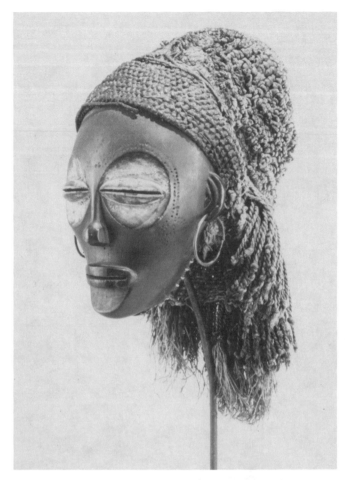

Masks are a part of the many traditional African cultures. This mask was made by the Chekwe peoples of Zaire and Angola.

*Courtesy of Jeffrey Ploskonka, Elisofan Archives, National Museum of African Art*

## Activity 4

A.  **Write to the National Museum of African Art, 950 Independence Avenue, S.W., Washington, D.C. 20560. Ask about:**

- art for special ceremonies, including religious art
- art for everyday use
- art stamped on cloth
- *Kente* cloth
- special art of African children

## B.    Some World-Famous People in African History

Conduct an investigation with a classmate or your class group. See how many of the clues 1 to 13 you can match with the names on the list. Check an encyclopedia and the library. Write your answers in order on a sheet of paper.

Jomo Kenyatta

Nelson Mandela

Julius Nyerere

Léopold Senghor

Archbishop Desmond
   Tutu

Patrice Lumumba

Ladysmith Black
   Mambazo

Albert Schweitzer

Christiaan Barnard

Kipchoge Keino

Miriam Makeba

Kwame Nkrumah

Haile Selassie

1.    South African leader; Nobel Peace Prize winner in 1984
2.    First prime minister of Kenya after independence (called *Mzee*, title of respect in Swahili)
3.    Emperor of Ethiopia, 1930-1974
4.    Civil rights leader in South Africa; imprisoned for many years and released in 1990
5.    Doctor who performed the first heart-transplant operation
6.    First president of Tanzania (he translated Shakespeare's plays into Swahili)
7.    First president of Ghana
8.    Poet, teacher, and political leader from French-speaking part of Africa (Senegal)
9.    Kenyan distance runner; won the goal medal at the 1968 and 1972 Olympic Games
10.    South African singer of black African songs
11.    South African music group
12.    First president of Zaire
13.    French doctor who ran a hospital in Africa; received the Nobel Peace Prize in 1952

## C.    Some Important Places in Sub-Saharan Africa

Look at a map of Africa. Locate each of these cities and tell what country it is in.

| | | | |
|---|---|---|---|
| Addis Ababa | Dar es Salaam | Johannesburg | Nairobi |
| Cape Town | Dakar | Kinshasa | Pretoria |

The elephant, a protected species in much of East Africa, is a frequent victim of illegal hunting.

*Courtesy of Eliot Elisofon, Elisofon Archives, National Museum of African Art*

# Africa's Gifts, continued

### Majestic Animals

Wildlife draws many visitors to East Africa each year.

You have probably seen some of these animals in a zoo. In Africa, they live in their natural home (habitat).

African governments have set aside large land reserves for these animals. One of them is the Serengeti National Park near Mount Kilimanjaro. It covers five thousand square miles!

Some of the animals that can be seen there include elephants, rhinoceroses, lions, gorillas, leopards, buffaloes, zebras, gazelles, hyenas, giraffes, and chimpanzees.

A journey or expedition into the animal areas is called a *safari*. Some safaris are for hunting and some are for taking pictures. People must have special permission from the government to enter the wildlife reserves. Only a few animals can be hunted and only at certain times. However, poachers (illegal hunters) continue to kill elephants, rhinoceroses, and other animals in order to get furs, tusks, and horns.

People around the world are interested in preserving wildlife. Explain the motto "Extinction is forever."

| Activity 5

**More than eight hundred languages are spoken in Africa. Some of them are:**

- Afrikaans [ahfri**kahns**]
- Akan [**ahk**han]
- Hausa [**how**zah]
- Igbo *or* Ibo [**ee**bo]
- Kikongo [kee**kohn**goh]
- Kiluba [kee**loo**bah]
- Lingala [leen**gah**lah]
- Shona [shoh**nah**]
- Xhosa [**koh**sah]
- Yoruba [**yoh**roobah]
- Zulu [**zoo**loo]

Find out where each of the languages on the list is spoken. Find out the names of other African languages.

# East African Foods

Have you ever tasted plantains? samusas? rice pancakes? meat curry? These are all examples of East African foods.

African cooking is rich in fresh fruits and vegetables. Soups and stews are also popular.

Have you ever seen plantains in the supermarket? Did you think they were bananas? They are related to bananas but they must be cooked before you eat them. Do they look different from bananas? They are usually bigger and their skin is thicker. They grow in warm, tropical countries just as bananas do.

Try this easy recipe for dessert. It serves four people.

---

**Recipe to Try**

## Baked Plantains

*Ingredients*

4 large ripe plantains

$^1/_2$ cup brown sugar

$^3/_4$ teaspoon cinnamon

$^1/_4$ cup melted butter
margarine

*Instructions*

1. Set oven on 350°F.

2. Wash the plantains and cut them in half lengthwise. Do not peel them.

3. Place the plantains in a shallow baking dish, cut sides up.

4. Cover them with the mixture of brown sugar, cinnamon, and melted butter or margarine.

5. Cover the pan and bake for 35 minutes or until plantains are soft.

---

To find out about other African foods, check in your library.

## Topics for Discussion and Review

1. Discuss the probable origins of the Swahili language. Why does it include words borrowed from other languages? Which languages?
2. Name the countries where Swahili is the official language. Name other countries where it is spoken.
3. With your class, partner, or group, conduct a discussion of why English and French are important languages in Africa.
4. Name as many African languages as you can.
5. Prepare a quiz for your class that includes questions about:
   a. a world-famous person from Africa
   b. an interesting African city

# Activities and Projects

1. African Americans are descended from the people of Africa. Investigate the work of the writer Alex Haley in tracing his roots to Africa. Prepare a report for the class. Include information about how Haley's ancestors and other Africans were brought to America as slaves.
2. Investigate a famous African American. Prepare questions for the class. See if the class can determine who the "mystery person" is.
3. Investigate masks in African art. Make a mask and write an explanation of its meaning. (Write for information to National Museum of African Art, 950 Independence Ave., S.W., Washington, D.C. 20560.)
4. Topics to read and report about:
   - NASA satellite named *Uhuru* (Write to NASA Headquarters, Washington, D.C. 20546.)
   - Stanley and Livingstone
   - the city of Timbuktu [timbuk**too**]
   - ancient African kingdoms, such as Mali
   - countries of West Africa where French is spoken

# CHAPTER FIFTEEN

# EXPLORING LATIN,
## ANCIENT ROME,
## AND ITS PEOPLE

# Salvete!

## Introducing Latin

A traveler lands in ancient Rome in a time machine. The traveler sees
a boy and a girl on the street. The boy is wearing a *tunic;* the girl, a
*stola.*

The girl says: *Salve, quis es?*

The boy says: *Marcus sum. Salve!*

Explore the first part of this Latin chapter and you will be able to
join the conversation.

Study the chapter pages that tell how to pronounce the Latin words
spoken by the girl and the boy.

## A Language Called Latin

Most of the languages you are exploring in this book are still spoken
in some part of the world. Latin *was* spoken in ancient Rome and the
Western Mediterranean until about twelve hundred years ago.

There is at least one place in the world today where official papers or documents are written in Latin. This is Vatican City, an independent state located in Rome. It is the headquarters of the Roman Catholic Church.

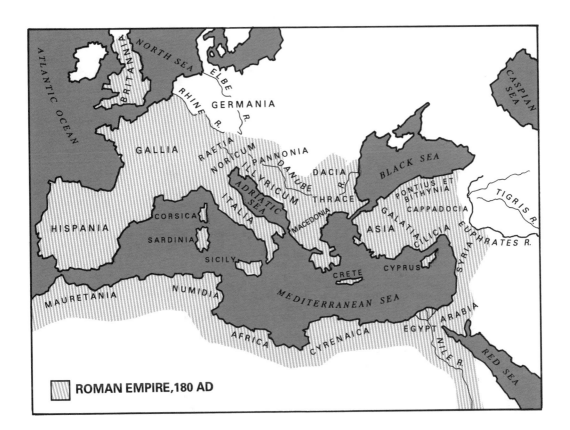

ROMAN EMPIRE, 180 AD

Latin is used in many legal documents and on national, state, and university seals. Doctors use Latin abbreviations when they write prescriptions.

Even though Latin is not usually spoken today, several languages come from Latin. What are the "children of Latin"? Remember the Romance languages (languages that come from the ancient Romans)? See if you can name them. Check chapter 4.

Over half of the English vocabulary is derived from Latin. In addition, when we speak English, we are frequently using *pure* Latin words.

You may wish to study Latin later in school. Knowing Latin words and how the language works is a useful tool for learning many other languages. Many Latin words have become *roots* in English, and we use them to form thousands of new words. You would be ahead of the game!

### What Does Latin Look Like?

Latin is all around us. Follow these directions and you will see examples of it.

1. Look at a penny or quarter. Find *E pluribus unum.* This motto also appears on the Great Seal of the U.S.

E Pluribus Unum
*(Out of many, one)*

2. Look at a cereal box, can of soup, or other packaged food. Find *lb.* This is the abbreviation for the Latin word *libra,* a measure of weight, a pound.
3. Look at a television schedule. You see A.M. and P.M. These are abbreviations for *ante meridiem* and *post meridiem. Meridiem* is noon.
4. *Etc.* is the abbreviation for Latin *et cetera* ("and the other things"). Latin is used on money, various consumer products, timetables, *etc.*
5. Look at an advertisement for an electronics store. *Video* is another word for "television." *Video* means "I see" in Latin.

## Activity 1

A.   As you learn Latin terms and their definitions, copy them in your notebook to start a Latin reference guide. You can begin with the terms you just learned. Divide your guide alphabetically so that you may add words later.

B.   Look up state seals in an encyclopedia. Most of the states have mottoes in Latin. List at least five of them with their translations.

## English Words with Latin Roots

We have seen some examples of pure Latin words used in English, such as *et cetera* and *video*.

There are many more words that are English but have Latin *roots*. Example: *aqua*lung, *aqua*rium, *aqua*tic. All of these words are related to *water. Aqua* is the part of the word that gives the basic meaning. It is the root.

*Aqua* in Latin, then, must mean "water."

## Activity 2

**Find the Latin Root**

With this book in hand, go to an unabridged dictionary in your school library or find an abridged dictionary that explains the origin of each word.

Helpful hint: In the dictionary you will usually find this information in brackets [ ] after the word and before the definition. It may also tell you which language the word came from.

Find the main *root* of each word listed below. Write the Latin *root* and the *meaning* of the English word on your paper.

| *Word* | *Latin Root* | *Meaning of the English Word* |
|---|---|---|
| **cent**ury | | |
| **un**it | | |
| **terr**estrial | | |
| **ocul**ist | | |

This arch was built in Rome
by the emperor Constantine.
Find out when it was built
and why.

*Courtesy of the Italian
Government Travel Office*

# Helpful Hints for Pronunciation of Latin Words

Latin words are easy to pronounce. The vowels can have different sounds, just as they do in English. These are called *long* and *short*. The consonants are similar to consonants in English. Keep these pronunciation hints in mind.

## Vowels

| *Long* | *Short* |
|---|---|
| *a* as in f*a*ther | *a* as in *a*bout |
| *e* as in th*ey* | *e* as in m*e*t |
| *i* as in m*ee*t | *i* as in s*i*t |
| *o* as in l*o*ne | *o* as in *o*ff |
| *u* as in c*oo*l | *u* as in f*u*ll |

## Consonants

*c*—always a *k* sound
*g*—always hard, as in *g*irl
*j*—sounds like *y* as in *y*ou
*qu*—always like *kw* as in *qu*ick
*s*—always like *s* as in *s*ay, never like *z*
*v*—like *w*

## A Special Vowel Combination

*ae*—sounds like the *ie* in *pie*.

(The famous Roman general's name was *Caesar*, pronounced [**kie**sahr] in Latin.)

If you study Latin later, you will learn more vowel combinations.

Here are some Latin words you will be using in the next section, "Let's Speak Latin!" Practice pronouncing them so you and a classmate can perform the skit in activity 3.

| *Latin Word* | *How It Sounds* | *Meaning* |
|---|---|---|
| salvete | [sahl**way**tay] | hello (to more than one person |
| salve | [**sahl**way] | hello (to one person) |
| Cornelia | [kor**nay**leea] | girl's name |
| sum | [sum] (as in *fu*ll) | I am |
| quis? | [kwis] | who? |
| es | [ehs] | are you |
| est | [ehst] | is |
| puer | [**poo**air] | boy |
| Marcus | [**mahr**kus] | boy's name |
| amici | [ah**mee**kee] | friends |
| Romani | [row**mah**nee] | Romans |
| valete | [wa**lay**tay] | good-bye (to more than one person) |
| fiat | [**fee**aht] | OK (let it be done) |
| agis | [**ah**gis] | you do, act |
| gratias | [grah**tee**ahs] | thanks |

# Let's Speak Latin! (Latine colloquamur)

You have just landed in ancient Rome in your time machine. You see a boy and a girl on the street. The boy is wearing a *tunic* and the girl, a *stola*. They are excited to see a visitor from another century!

Cornelia:  Salve! Cornelia sum. Quis es?

You:  [Your name] sum. Salve! Quis est puer?

Cornelia:  Marcus est.

You:  Salvete! Valete, amici Romani!

What did you and Cornelia say? Read the meaning of the conversation below.

| | |
|---|---|
| Cornelia: | Hello! I'm Cornelia. Who are you? |
| You: | I'm [your name]. Hello! Who is the boy? |
| Cornelia: | That's Marcus. |
| You: | Hello! Good-bye, Roman friends! |

## Activity 3

**With a partner, practice acting out the above skit several times. Then present it to the class.**

## A Polite Conversation

Practice this skit with a classmate.

| | |
|---|---|
| You: | Salve!* |
| Classmate: | Salve! |
| You: | Latine colloquamur. |
| Classmate: | Fiat. (OK.) |
| You: | Quid agis? (How are you?) |
| Classmate: | Satis bene, gratias. (Pretty well, thanks.) |
| You: | Vale!* |
| Classmate: | Vale! |

## Activity 4

**Find the Latin word in the conversation related to these English words:**

- grateful
- satisfied
- agitate

Write the Latin words on your paper.

---

*Use *salve* and *valete* when you speak to one person, and *salvete* and *valete* when you speak to more than one person.

# Learning to Count in Latin

Say the numbers from 1 to 10 in Latin.

| Number | Latin | How It Sounds |
|---|---|---|
| 1 | unus | [**oo**noos] |
| 2 | duo | [**doo**o] |
| 3 | tres | [trace] |
| 4 | quattuor | [**kwaht**wor] |
| 5 | quinque | [**kwink**way] |
| 6 | sex | [sex] |
| 7 | septem | [**sep**tem] |
| 8 | octo | [**ok**toh] |
| 9 | novem | [**noh**wem] |
| 10 | decem | [**dek**em] |

The Forum in Rome was once a great gathering place for the people of the city. Find out more about the forum and the activities that went on there.

*Courtesy of the Italian Government Travel Office*

## Activity 5

**The English words below all come from (are derived from) Latin numbers. Tell which Latin number name each is derived from. Then use each in a sentence.**

unified

duet

September

octagon

decimals

## Roman Numerals

Of course, you know that the numbers we use in everyday life are Arabic numbers. The ancient Romans used letters as numbers. We call these Roman numerals. In the modern world, Roman numerals are used on the faces of some clocks and watches, for divisions in an outline, and sometimes for dates on buildings. Arabic numbers are used in most other instances.

### Roman Numerals You Should Know

*1-10*
I, II, III, IV, V, VI, VII, VIII, IX, X

*11-20*
XI, XII, XIII, XIV, XV, XVI, XVII, XVIII, XIX, XX

*30, 40, 50*
XXX, XL, L

*60, 70, 80, 90*
LX, LXX, LXXX, XC

*100*
C = centum [**ken**toom] (remember *century?*)

*500*
D = quingenti [kwin**gen**ti]

*1,000*
M 5 mille [**mee**lay] (remember *millimeter?*)

### Rules for Roman Numerals

1. A smaller number *preceding* a larger number is subtracted from that number.
   IV = 4 (1 subtracted from 5 equals 4)
   IX = 9 (1 subtracted from 10 equals 9)
2. A smaller number *following* a larger number is added to that number.
   LV = 55 (5 added to 50 equals 55)
   CX = 110 (10 added to 100 equals 110)

What is the Arabic number for VII?
What is the Arabic number for DC?

## Activity 6

**A.** **What do the following Roman numerals mean? Refer to the "Rules for Roman Numerals."**

XIX            XXX            XCI            MDCCLXXVI

**B.** **On your paper, write these dates in Roman numerals.**

1492      1789      1941      1968      1990      2000

**C.** **Have you noticed the dates on movies? Roman numerals are sometimes used to show the year when a film was made. Be sure to watch for the date the next time you go to the movies.**

The Piazza Navona is a famous square in modern Rome. In ancient times, it was a place where races were held, which accounts for its oval shape.

*Courtesy of the Italian Government Travel Office*

# Everyday Latin Connections

Many of our everyday words, expressions, and names of people and places are really Latin or derived from Latin.

Some occupations or professions use Latin in some way; for example, health occupations and the practice of law.

In what way does a pharmacist use Latin? Think about it! As you continue to read this chapter, the answer will become obvious to you.

### Months of the Year

The English names for the months of the year come directly from ancient Roman times. The Romans had devised a calendar. You may wish to do a special report on this calendar for your class.

Let's see how the names of the months come from Latin.

## Activity 7

**Here are some facts that relate to our calendar. On a sheet of paper, write the name of the month that corresponds to each fact.**

1. The Roman god of war was Mars.
2. The first Roman emperor was Augustus.
3. The Roman god of gates and doors was Janus. He had two faces—one looking forward, the other looking back. This is the month when people look back and look ahead.
4. One of the most famous generals of Rome was Julius Caesar.
5. The Latin verb *aperire* (to open) also referred to spring, when the earth "opens" and plants start to grow.
6. In Roman mythology, Maia was the daughter of Atlas and the mother of the god Mercury.
7. Junius (or Iunius) was the name of a famous family clan in ancient Rome.
8. In the original Roman calendar, the year began with March. Name the months that were the seventh, eighth, ninth, and tenth months in that calendar. When January and February were added, the calendar increased to twelve months. The names of the last four months were no longer correct, but the world has kept them as they were!

### Latin in the World of Science and Technology

Many words in science and technology have their origins in Latin.

## Activity 8

A.  **The planets were named after the gods and goddesses of Roman mythology. Name the planets of our solar system.**

**B.** **Scientists are doing research in these areas:**

> *terra* (terrestrial)
> *sol* (solar)
> *luna* (lunar)
> *mare* (marine)

**Give the meanings of the Latin words above.**

## Latin in the World of Medicine

Do you know someone who wants to become a doctor? Knowing Latin is a valuable tool for medical students because the names of parts of the body including bones are Latin. Some examples are the tibia, the ulna, and the patella.

Many doctors use certain Latin abbreviations when writing prescriptions. The pharmacist at the drugstore knows what they mean and is able to fill prescriptions correctly. Doctors all over the world can use these same abbreviations no matter what language they speak.

## Latin and Law

Almost all documents that lawyers use contain some Latin phrases.

Because most of our Founding Fathers had studied Latin, the United States inherited many law and government expressions from the ancient Romans.

## Latin Mottoes

What organizations use Latin mottoes? Clubs, states, universities, schools, classes, and businesses! You saw a Latin motto earlier in this chapter. Here are more Latin mottoes:

- Semper paratus
- Semper fidelis
- Mens sana in corpore sano

See if you can match the meanings below with the mottoes above.
- "A sound mind in a sound body" (YMCA)
- "Always faithful" (U.S. Marine Corps)
- "Always prepared" (U.S. Coast Guard)

## Latin Expressions

You may also be familiar with some of these Latin expressions:

- Carpe diem—"Seize the day (opportunity)" (Go for it!)
- Tempus fugit—"Time flies"
- Labor omnia vincit—"Work conquers all"
- Amor omnia vincit—"Love conquers all"
- Veni, vidi, vici—"I came, I saw, I conquered"*
- persona non grata—"unwanted person"

When might you use each of these expressions?

---

| Activity 9 |
|---|

**A. With the help of your classmates and the approval of your teacher, devise a class motto in Latin, using the words you already know.**

**B. A Few More Latin Expressions**

Read each sentence. On a sheet of paper, copy the Latin expression and tell what it means. An unabridged dictionary will help.

- Washington High School was his *alma mater.*
- The newspaper included a column labeled *in memoriam.*
- The hospital conducted a *post mortem* examination.
- If you're not a sailor, you may prefer *terra firma.*
- It was their school *versus* our school!

## Prefix Review

Here is a list of some common prefixes in English. Did you know that these are really Latin words? If you know what each prefix means, it will help you know the meaning of the word it is part of.

| Prefix | Meaning | Prefix | Meaning |
|---|---|---|---|
| ab- | from, away from | post- | after |
| circum- | around | sub- | under |
| con- | against, or with | super- | above |
| inter- | between | trans- | across |
| non- | not | | |

---

*Words of Julius Caesar after winning a short war in Anatolia (modern Turkey).

### Build a word!

- Take a word *root:* scribe, script, sense, sent, stance, vent.
- Put a prefix in front of it.
- Check a dictionary if you're not sure.

**Example:** *circum* + *navigate* = *circumnavigate*. What does the new word mean?

## Abbreviation Review

Match the Latin abbreviation in the right column to its correct definition in the left column. Write the answer on a sheet of paper.

1. for example                           A.D.
2. that is                               lb.
3. in the year of Our Lord              e.g.
   (*after* Christ)                      P.S.
4. and others                            et al.
5. before noon                           P.M.
6. after noon                            etc.
7. postscript                            i.e.
8. pound                                 A.M.
9. and so forth

Copy each Latin expression next to its abbreviation on your paper.

Anno Domini
exempli gratia
et alii
et cetera
ante meridiem
libra
post scriptum
post meridiem
id est

## Latin and the Constellations

con—with
stella—star
-tion—quality of
Constellation: a group of stars *appearing* to be together

When the ancient Romans and Greeks looked up at the night sky, they imagined the stars formed the shapes of mythological figures, and they created stories about these characters.

The Big Bear and Little Bear are probably the most famous. Have you heard of their Latin names? *Ursa* (Bear) *Major* (bigger) and *Ursa Minor* (smaller).

In the English-speaking world, we also call them

B _ _ D _ p p _ _ and L _ _ _ _ _ D _ p p _ _

At the tip of *Ursa Minor's* tail is a famous star:

P _ _ _ _ i s

You may wish to investigate how the Big Bear and Little Bear came to be, according to Roman mythology.

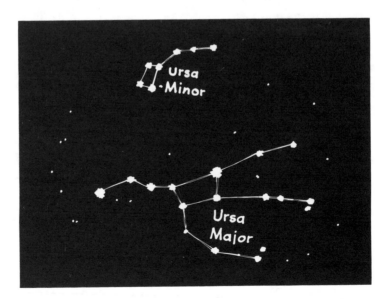

This is only one example of a constellation. You may wish to find out more about the "stories of the stars." See "Activities and Projects" at the end of this chapter.

# A Song in Latin

## Mica, Mica Parva Stella

This Latin version of "Twinkle, Twinkle Little Star" is sung by Latin students all over the United States. See how many words you recognize as you sing the song with your class.

Mica, mica, parva stella!
Tu es vero satis bella,
Lucens super hoc mundo,
Velut gemma in caelo.
Mica, mica, parva stella!
Tu es vero satis bella.

**INDEX VERBORUM:**

| | |
|---|---|
| **bella**—pretty | **parva**—small, little |
| **caelo**—sky | **satis**—quite |
| **gemma**—jewel | **stella**—star |
| **hoc**—this | **tu**—you |
| **lucens**—shining | **velut**—just as |
| **mica**—glitter | **vero**—indeed |
| **mundo**—mundo | |

## Pronunciation Hints

lucens [**loo**kens]
caelo [**ky**loh]
velut [**way**lut]

Check the pronunciation section in this chapter to help you pronounce other words you may not be sure of.

# Topics for Discussion and Review

1. Show in as many ways as you can why Latin is not "dead."
2. Why is the learning of Latin important?
3. Does your city, county, or state have a Latin motto? What is it? Be sure that you can pronounce it and that you know its meaning and history.
4. Name the languages that come from Latin.

# Activities and Projects

1.  Develop a report on the Roman calendar, including a chart.
2.  Prepare an oral report about one of these historic Romans:

    Julius Caesar                Virgil
    Augustus                     Cicero

3.  Make a study of the well-known constellations. Using draw-ings, explain them to your class. Consult your science text, as well as the encyclopedia. Visit an observatory or a plane-tarium, if there is one near where you live.
4.  Put on a fashion show featuring you and your classmates as Roman gods and goddesses. Prepare a script for the announcer to read while each god or goddess appears before the class in appropriate costume.

# Mystery Words: Latin-English Connections

Because Latin has so many connections to English, here is a special Mystery Word page for you to tackle. Check an unabridged dictionary.

**Mystery Word 1**

Find the Latin words in this English word. Write them on your paper with their meanings.

**Mystery Word 2**

K-9 Corps

How did this name originate? What is the Latin connection?

**Mystery Word 3**

muscle

What is the connection between a *mouse* and a *muscle?*

**Mystery Word 4**

SPQR

Where do we see this combination of letters and to what do they refer?

# EXPLORING ANCIENT GREEK
## AND THE ANCIENT GREEK WORLD

# Χαîρε*

## Introducing Ancient Greece

Of all the civilizations of the ancient world, that of the Greeks is one of the most admired. We look with amazement on the achievements of the Greeks in architecture, sculpture, and literature. One reason these people were able to accomplish so much was that beauty, art, and literature were very important in their culture. The idea of democracy also evolved in ancient Greece. The word *democracy* is Greek in origin. The Greeks produced ideas that influence people's thinking to this day. Some ancient Greek scholars studied in Egypt, where they learned many things from the Egyptian civilization, which they used in new ways.

---

*This is the ancient Greek word for hello (pronounced "**hiray**").

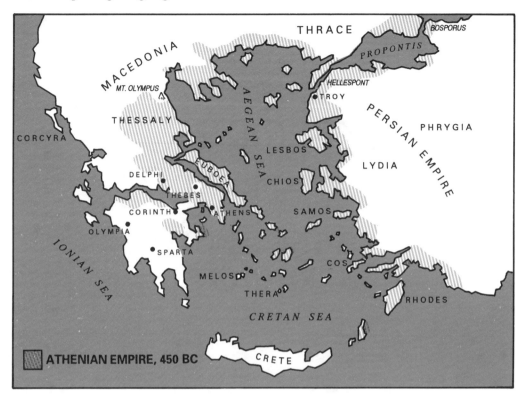

Look at a map of Europe, locate Greece, and be able to explain where it is.

Modern science is based on the Greek idea of solving problems by reasoning. The ancient Greeks believed in the *golden mean*—everything in moderation; nothing to excess—the balanced life of mind and body.

Remember that the Greeks started the Olympic games in 776 B.C. They were held in honor of the god Zeus, who they thought lived on Mount Olympus. The games were held every four years and featured athletics, poetry, and dance. Today's Olympic Games are part of our Greek heritage.

Did you know that the word *athlete* comes from Greek? An athlete was one who competed for an award.

## Greek, an Ancient Language

The Greek language dates back at least to 1400 B.C. Do you see, then, that it is more than three thousand years old? Some people believe that a system of Greek writing existed centuries before 1000 B.C. By 800 B.C., the Greeks had adopted the Phoenician alphabet, which we still use today, as modified by the Romans. The influence of this language on other languages and cultures of the world was enormous!

The Latin language borrowed from the Greek language. Even though Roman armies conquered Greece (between 140 B.C. and 27 B.C.), it can be argued that Greece conquered Rome. The Romans learned to appreciate the great ideas, the art, the poems, and the stories of the Greeks.

Many Romans went to Greece to study, just as some Greeks had gone to Egypt. Many Greeks went to Rome as teachers. Cicero, the famous Roman orator, studied in Greece as a young man. Some of the great Greek works have lasted over two thousand years!

Today about ten million people speak modern Greek as their native language. Modern Greek differs in many ways from the ancient language.

The Parthenon in Athens is one of the monuments of ancient Greece. Dating from the fifth century B.C., it is a temple dedicated to the goddess Athena.

*Courtesy of the Greek National Tourist Organization*

## Activity 1

**A special kind of story that tells about heroes, gods, and goddesses and their great adventures is called an *epic*. Find out the name of a famous storyteller of ancient Greece.**

**Hint:** His two well-known poems are *The Iliad* and *The Odyssey.* After reading in the encyclopedia about *The Iliad* and *The Odyssey,* write a brief paragraph on each.

# The Ancient Greek Alphabet

The letters of the Greek alphabet are listed below with their Roman alphabet equivalents. Notice that our word *alphabet* is made up of the names of the first two letters in the Greek alphabet.

| *Greek* | | *Letter* | *English* |
|---|---|---|---|
| Capital Letter | Small Letter | *Name* | *"Sound"* |
| A | A | alpha | a |
| B | β | beta | b |
| Γ | γ | gamma | g |
| Δ | δ | delta | d |
| E | ε | epsilon | e as in met |
| Z | ζ | zeta | z |
| H | η | eta | ay |
| Θ | θ | theta | th |
| I | ι | iota | i |
| K | κ | kappa | k |
| Λ | λ | lambda | l |
| M | μ | mu | m |
| N | ν | nu | n |
| Ξ | ξ | xi | x or ks |
| O | o | omicron | o |
| Π | π | pi | p |
| P | ρ | rho | r |
| Σ | σ | sigma | s |
| T | τ | tau | t |
| Y | υ | upsilon | yew |
| Φ | φ | phi | f or ph |
| X | χ | chi | kh |
| Ψ | ψ | psi | ps |
| Ω | ω | omega | oh |

Have you noticed which letters do not appear in the English sound column? You are correct if you said *c, v, j, q,* and *w.*

The classical Greek alphabet is used in formulas in mathematics, science, and technology. If you study advanced math or engineering, the Greek alphabet will become a useful tool in your work.

The Greek writing on the Rosetta Stone was the key to understanding Egyptian hieroglyphics. Scholars used the Greek on the stone to figure out what was written in hieroglyphics, which until then could not be read.

*Reproduced by Courtesy of the Trustees of the British Museum*

## Activity 2

### A. "Pursue the Facts" Game

**Pursue these facts about the uses of the Greek alphabet in English. Each answer is worth 10 points. See if you can earn 80 points. Write your answer on a sheet of paper.**

1.  gamma rays                     What are they?
    Mississippi Delta              Why is this so named?
    I don't care one iota!         What does this mean?
    $A = \pi r^2$                  Explain what it means.
    A to $\Omega$                  Explain what it means.

2.  *Societies, Fraternities, Sororities*
    $\Phi$BK                       What does it mean?
    $\Sigma$X                      What is it?
    AZ$\Delta$                     What is it?

**B.    Greek Place Names in the United States**

Some well-known places in our country were named after places in Greece. *Athens* is the capital of Greece. Find a city called Athens on a map of the United States. How about Atlanta? Ithaca? Ypsilanti? What state is each city in? Find out if there is a city with a Greek name in your state.

# Greek Roots

You have already seen some English words that were built on Greek roots. Many words in the areas of science, the professions, and everyday life have Greek roots. You probably know several words that come from Greek; you might say that you have been using Greek for years without realizing it! Once you understand the Greek roots in words you know, you will find it much easier to figure out the meanings of words you have never seen before.

## Activity 3

**A.    Greek Words in the World of Work**

Many occupations use words that come from Greek.

Look at the list of words below. Give another word that uses the same underlined root. Use the words in a discussion with your team or partner, or write sentences on your paper. If you write sentences, try to write a connected paragraph.

**Health Words**
*derm*atitis
*osteo*path
*card*iac

**Technology Words**
*kilo*watt
*heli*port
tele*scope*

**Science/Mathematics Words**
*poly*gon
*baro*meter
*hydro*gen

Theater was important in ancient Greece, and the remains of Greek theaters are still impressive. Can you find the names of some ancient Greek playwrights?

*Courtesy of the Greek National Tourist Organization*

## B.    Greek Roots in Fields of Study

The ancient Greeks organized learning into fields of study. Many of these fields use the same names today. An example is *biology.* What will you study when you take biology? The Greek word *bios* is your clue.

   If you know the meanings of several Greek roots, it will be easy for you to learn many new English words having to do with science and other fields of study. A few are listed below. Use your dictionary. Supply the answers on a sheet of paper.

| 1. *Greek Roots* | *Meaning of the Root* | *English Derivatives* |
|---|---|---|
| aer | air | _____ |
| anthropos | human | anthropology |
| astron | _____ | astronomy |
| auto | self | _____ |
| bios | _____ | biology |
| ge | earth | _____ |
| micros | _____ | microscope |
| phone | sound | telephone |
| theos | a god | theology |
| photon | light | _____ |

2.    Choose two of the English derivatives from part 1. Use each one in a sentence.

3. Name five fields of study whose names come from Greek. The descriptions below will help you. Write the names on a sheet of paper.

- If I go into this field, I will learn about care of the hair, cutting, shampooing, and other beauty needs.
- In this field, I will be a doctor who is an eye specialist.
- In this field, I will study living things.
- In this field, I will study rocks and the earth's surface.
- As a scientist in this field, I will study human beings.

## C.  Some Word Families from Greek

1. On a sheet of paper, write the words that belong in the blanks.

Words with the Greek root *graph* (writing):
biography          life-writing
geography          _____-writing
photography        light-writing
autograph          _____-writing
telegraph          at-a-distance-writing

2. Define each of the following.

Words with the Greek root *tele* (far off):
telephone       telephoto
telescope       teletype
telepathy       telecommunications

3. On a sheet of paper, write the words that belong in the blanks.

Words with the Greek root *logos* (word, study):
biology        study of _____
physiology     study of the body
zoology        study of _____

4. On a sheet of paper, write the words that belong in the blanks.

Words with the Greek root *metron* (a measure):
meter          measure of length
thermometer    measure of _____
pedometer      measure of _____

These columns are part of the ancient city of Mycenae. The modern name is spelled Mikínai. Find Mycenae or Mikínai on a map of Greece.

*Courtesy of A. Cannon*

## Topics for Discussion and Review

1. Talk about what the modern world owes to ancient Greece.
2. How old is the Greek language? How many people speak modern Greek today?
3. Describe the classical Greek alphabet and its uses today in the English-speaking world.
4. Be prepared to explain to a friend the original meaning of the word *democracy*.
5. List five Greek roots that are used in English. Give the meaning of each root and an English word containing that root.
6. Find out who Hippocrates was. In what field is he honored?

## Activities and Projects

1. Choose one of these topics. Prepare a report with a partner or a group.

   - Greek games and festivals
   - Greek architecture
   - Trojan War
   - origin of the Olympic Games
   - Homer

2. Greek and Roman mythology have much in common. Make a list of Roman gods and goddesses and find out their *Greek* names.

   **Example:**
   Jupiter (Latin), Zeus [zoos] (Greek)

3. Make a poster for your class illustrating a "word family" derived from a Greek root. Illustrate as many English words as you can that contain this root.

   **Example:**
   *tele*—distant: television, telegram, etc.

4. Make a poster for an English class in your school. Add a Greek prefix to the endings below. Illustrate the meaning of each word on your poster.

   -ology / -phone / -graph / -scope / -pathy / -crat

5. Write a plan for a tour of Greece. List places to see and tell what is special about each.

---

### Mystery Words

1. What is the true meaning of *school* from the original Greek word? (You will be surprised!)
2. If you know the meaning of *democrat,* you should be able to figure out *autocrat* and *plutocrat*!

---

### A "Fun" Word:

### TRISKAIDEKAPHOBIA

This is not a Greek word, and it is not a standard English word. It was coined many years ago by Americans playing games with Greek roots. Can you figure out what the intended meaning is?

**Clues:**

TRI-              DEKA-              -PHOBIA

# Index

Africa
  Arabic-speaking regions, 171–73
  famous cities, 205
  foods, 207–8
  languages, variety of, 198, 207
  national parks, 206
  recipe, 208
  Swahili-speaking regions, 196–97
  world-famous people, 205
Afrikaans (language), 207
Akan (language), 207
*Alouette* (French Canadian song),
    88
alphabets, 44, 129–30, 174–75, 187,
    228–29, 230
  Arabic, 174–75
  Cyrillic, 129–30
  Greek (Ancient), 230
  Hebrew, 187
  Spanish, 57–58
amateur radio, 14–17
  Morse Code, 14, 16
American Sign Language, 13–14
Angles, 27–28
Arabic language, 171–84
  alphabet, 44, 174–75
  Arabesque, 176
  Arabic words in English, 174
  calligraphy, 176
  countries where spoken, 171–73

greetings, 177–78
  history of, 176–77
  influence on Spanish, 177
  language facts, 175–76
  numbers, 178–79
  Semitic family, 176
  writing, 174–76
  zero (origin), 179
Arabic-speaking countries, 171–74
  Arab centers of learning (historic),
    177
  Crusades, 177
  famous places, 182
  folktales (Arabian Nights), 181
  foods, 181
  Islam, 180
  map, 172
  Moors, 177
  Qur'an, 180
Astronomy, 11, 220, 224
  planets, 11

Balto-Slavic branch (Indo-European),
    42–43
  Bulgarian, 42–43, 127
  Lithuanian, 42–43
  Polish, 42–43, 127
  Russian, 42–43, 126–42
  Slovak, 42–43, 127
Bantu (language family), 42, 199

Braille, 14
Burmese (language), 42
Burundi, 196

Cajun, 79
calligraphy, 148–49, 166–67, 176
Canada, 78–79
careers, in foreign languages, 8
Caxton, William, 32
Celts, 24–25, 27
China, 158–70
    cooking, 169
    festivals and holidays, 164
    geography, 158–60
    history of, 160–63
    map, 159
    people and traditions, 163–64
Chinese language, 4, 42, 164–68
    background, 164–65
    characters, 166–68
    dialects, 167
    greetings, 168
    pronunciation, 165–68
    Sino-Tibetan, 42, 164
    writing, 166–67
*Cielito Lindo* (Mexican song), 67–68
communication, 2–4
    signs and symbols, 3, 9–17
    systems, 3, 13–17
Congo Republic, 196
Cyrillic (alphabet), 44, 129–30

Danes, 29
dialect, 167, 198
Dutch, 4, 38, 45

Egypt (ancient), 227, 231
Egypt (modern), 173
English language, 22–32
    French influence on, 31, 35, 80
    Germanic origin, 27–29, 42, 46

Great Britain, 22–32, 37–39
    history of, 22–32
    Indo-European, 22, 42, 45–46
    Latin influence on, 25–28, 219–24
    mixture of languages, 32
Esperanto, 17–21
    Children around the World, 20
    dialogue, 20–21
    Esperanto League for North
        America (ELNA), 20
    Zamenhof, Ludwig, 18–19

France, 74–77
    contributions, 76
    famous people, 76
    geography, 75
    map, 75
French language, 4, 30–31, 35,
        77–92
    Cajun/Creole, 79
    Canada, 78–79
    classroom expressions, 85
    dialogue, 84, 86
    French in U.S., 35, 79
    French words in English, 31, 80
    greetings, 83–84
    history of, 74
    influence on English language,
        30–31, 35, 80
    Latin origins, 74
    Louisiana, 79–80
    menu, 87
    numbers, 82
    other French-speaking regions,
        77–80
    pronunciation, 81, 90–91
    Romance language, 74
    song (*Alouette*), 88

German language, 93, 98–108
    days of the week, 100

foods, 104–5
German words in English, 98–101
Germans in the U.S., 98
greetings, 103
names of the months, 100
numbers, 102
Pennsylvania Dutch, 98
pronunciation, 101–2
regions where spoken, 93
song (*O Tannenbaum*), 106
Germanic languages, 27–28, 42–43, 46
Germany, 93
famous people, 96–97
geography of, 94–95
history of, 93–95
map, 94
Great Britain, 22–32, 37–39
Greece (Ancient), 227–29
democracy, 227
*Iliad*, 229
map, 228
mythology, 228, 229
*Odyssey*, 229
Olympic games, 228
Greek language (Ancient), 228–36
alphabet, 230
creating new English words, 232–34
Greek words and roots in English, 232–34
history of, 228–29
influence on Latin, 229
Phoenician alphabet, 228–29
science terms, 232–34
greetings
Arabic, 177–78
Chinese, 168
French, 83–84
German, 103
Hebrew, 188

Italian, 112–13
Japanese, 153
Latin, 215–16
Russian, 135–36
Spanish, 64–65

Hadrian's Wall, 25–26
Ham radio (amateur radio), 14–17
Hausa (language), 207
Hebrew language, 185–90
alphabet, 187
greetings, 188
Hebrew names, 190
Hebrew words in English, 190
numbers, 189
song (*Shalom Havayreem*), 194
Hindi, 42–43

Igbo (language), 207
Indo-European family, 22, 42–43, 45–46
Indo-Iranian branch (Indo-European), 42–43
Israel, 191–95
calendar, 193
history of, 191
holidays, 193
Judaism, Islam, Christianity, 191
map, 192
Italian language, 111–25
classroom exprassions, 115
days of the week, 114
foods, 121–23
greetings, 112–13
Italian words in English, 121
months of the year, 114–15
musical terms, 117
numbers, 116–17
piano, 117, 119
Romance language, 111
song (*Santa Lucia*), 120

Italic (Latin) branch (Indo-European), 42–43
Italy, 109–11
  famous Italians, 111
  map, 110, 211
  Renaissance, 109–10
  Rome, 109, 114, 117, 210, 214, 217, 219

Japan, 143–47
  festivals, 146
  foods, 153–55
  geography of, 143–144
  history of, 143–47
  map, 144
  recipe, 155
  tea ceremony, 146
Japanese language, 147–57
  Chinese influence on, 147–49
  greetings, 153
  hiragana, 147–49
  Japanese words from English, 152
  kanji, 147–50
  katakana, 147–49
  numbers, 150
  romaji, 147, 150, 151
  song (*Sakura, Sakura*), 156
Jutes, 27

Kenya, 196, 198
Kikongo (language), 207
Kiluba (language), 207
Kiswahili (language), 199
Korean (language), 4
Kwanzaa, 202

Lakota (language), 42
language tree (Indo-European), 43
Languages, 4
  alphabets, 44

computer, 3
importance of, 2–4
Indo-European, 42–43
invented (Esperanto), 17–21
study of, 7–8
Latin language, 26–27, 43, 210–226
  abbreviations, 212, 223
  constellations, 224
  dialogue/expressions, 215, 216
  greetings, 215–16
  legal terms, 221
  map, 211
  medical terms, 221
  mottoes, 221–22
  numbers, 217
  prefixes, 222
  pronunciation, 214–15
  Roman numerals, 218–19
  roots in English, 223
  science, 220–21
  song (*Mica, Mica, Parva Stella*), 225
  U.S. motto (*E pluribus unum*), 212
  Vatican City, 211
Lingala (language), 207
Lithuanian, 43

Malagasy Republic, 196
Malawi, 196
Mardi Gras, 35, 79
Mercury, 11
Mexico, 53–54, 55, 66
  Mexican Americans, 54
Morse Code, 14, 16
Mozambique, 196

Native American, 33–35, 42
  place names, 33–35
Normans, 29–31

Paris, 75, 76, 82, 85

Pennsylvania Dutch, 98

Persian (Farsi), 42–43

piano, origin of the, 119

pinyin, 165

place names (U.S.), origin of, 33–38

Portuguese (language), 42–43, 51

Puerto Rico, 54

Qur'an, 180

recipes, 155, 208

romaji, 147, 150, 151

Romans (Ancient), 210–226
   alphabet, 44
   calendar, 220
   conquest of Britain, 25
   mythology, 220, 224
   numerals, 218–19

Romanian, 42–43

Rome (Ancient), 210–226
   map, 211

Rosetta Stone, 231

Russia, 130–33
   famous people, 131, 137–38
   geography of, 131–32
   history of, 130–33
   landmarks, 130–33
   map, 128
   matryoshka dolls, 139
   Moscow, 132, 134
   St. Petersburg (Leningrad), 133

Russian language, 126–30, 134–37
   Cyrillic alphabet, 44, 129–30
   English words from Russian, 135
   greetings/other expressions,
     135–36
   numbers, 137
   Slavic language, 42
   song (*Volga Boatmen*), 140
   transliteration, 129, 130
   writing, 129, 130

Rwanda, 196

*Sakura, Sakura* (Japanese song), 156

Sanskrit language, 45–46

*Santa Lucia* (Italian song), 120

Saxons, 27–28

*Shalom Havayreem* (Hebrew song),
   194

Shona (language), 207

Signing, 13–14

Signs and symbols, 3–6, 9–17
   American Sign Language, 13–14
   astronomy, 11
   Braille, 14
   international traffic signs, 13
   mathematical symbols, 11
   Morse Code, 14, 16
   planets, 11
   science, 12
   theater, 11

Sino-Tibetan family, 42

Sioux language family, 42

Slavic branch (Indo-European),
   42–43

Somalia, 196

songs, 67–68, 88, 120, 140, 156, 194,
   225
   *Alouette*, 88
   *Cielito Lindo*, 67–68
   *Mica, Mica, Parva Stella*, 225
   *O Tannenbaum*, 106
   *Sakura, Sakura*, 166
   *Santa Lucia*, 120
   *Shalom Havayreem*, 194
   *Volga Boatmen*, 140

Spain, 50–52
   geography of, 50–52
   map, 52

Spanish language, 4, 36–37, 50–73
  alphabet, 57–58
  classroom expressions and objects,
    65–67
  days of week, 63
  greetings, 64–65
  Latin influence on, 50
  months, 63
  names in Spanish, 61
  numbers, 59–60
  place names in U.S., 36–37
  pronunciation, 71–73
  Romance language, 50
  song (*Cielito Lindo*), 67–68
  Spanish-speaking areas (in U.S.),
    54
  Spanish words in English, 55
  telling time, 62–63
Stonehenge, 23
Swahili language, 4, 196–202
  African regions where spoken
    (map), 196–97
  Arabic connections, 199
  Bantu family, 42, 199
  greetings/expressions, 199–200
  history of, 198–99
  Kwanzaa, 202–3
  map, 197
  numbers, 201

Tanzania, 196
Thai, 42
Tibetan, 42
transliteration, 129, 130

Uganda, 196

Vietnamese language, 4
*Volga Boatmen* (Russian song), 140

Xhosa (language), 207

Yoruba (language), 4, 207

Zaire (eastern), 196, 200
Zambia, 196
Zamenhof, Ludwig, 18–19
zero, origin of, 179
Zulu (language), 207

# Acknowledgments

The authors appreciate the linguistic assistance of the persons cited below in the writing of the chapters indicated.

| | |
|---|---|
| *Arabic* | Dr. Aref Abdul-Baki |
| *Chinese* | Claudine Ho and Stuart Sargent |
| *Esperanto* | Charlotte Kohrs, Beatrice Acers, and the Esperanto League for North America |
| *German* | Fred Schneider, Karen Martinez, and Esther Monke |
| *Greek* | Ioanna Papandreou |
| *Hebrew* | Dr. Ira Weiss, Isaac Yehiel, and Dr. Dallas C. Kennedy |
| *Japanese* | Yasuko Nainan |
| *Latin* | Salvatore Parlato |
| *Russian* | Julie Steimel and Douglas Cook |
| *Swahili* | Cheryl Escobar and Griselda Clemons |

The assistance of the following institutions and individuals is also acknowledged.

Anacostia Museum of the Smithsonian Institution
British Museum
David Kennedy Center for International Studies (Brigham Young University)
Embassy of Kenya
Embassy of Saudi Arabia
French Office of Tourism
German Information Center
Greek National Tourist Organization
Italian Government Travel Office
Lafayette Convention and Visitors Commission (Louisiana)
Maryland State Department of Transportation
Mexican Ministry of Tourism

Museum of African Art (Washington, D.C.)
National Zoological Park (Washington, D.C.)
Network of QSL Cards (Louisiana)
Permanent Mission of the Republic of Kenya to the United Nations
Puerto Rican Tourism Company
Rowland Company
St. Augustine Chamber of Commerce
Tourism Office of Spain (New York City)

Sonja Ailcea, the late Ann Beusch, Diana Brosnan, Edward L. Burns, Adrienne & Joel Cannon, Griselda Clemons, Jim Evans, Barbara Fretz, Pauline Grant, Nancy Hair, David & Sari Kaye, Dallas C. Kennedy, Elena Marra-Lopez, Joan Patterson, Jeri Perkins, Sahomi Sargent, Jim Sherwood, Linda Thompson, and Nancy Weigant.

We wish to acknowledge the help and support of our families.

Our greatest appreciation is expressed to Irma Nicholson McCafferty, our typist, whose dedication always exceeded the call of duty, and to Janet Battiste, our persevering editor.

# NTC ELEMENTARY LANGUAGE TEXTS
## AND MATERIAL

**Multilingual Resources**
Basic Vocabulary Builder
Practical Vocabulary Builder
Language Visuals
NTC Language Posters
NTC Language Puppets
NTC Language Learning Flash Cards

**Spanish**
¡Viva el español!
  Learning Systems A, B, C
  Converso mucho
  Ya converso más
  ¡Nos comunicamos!
Welcome to Spanish
  First Start in Spanish
  Moving Ahead in Spanish
Spanish for Young Americans
  Hablan los niños
  Hablan más los niños
  Bienvenidos
Diccionario Bilingüe Ilustrado
Mi primera fonética
Mi cuaderno Workbooks 1, 2, 3
Aprendamos español Picture
  Dictionary
Let's Learn Spanish Picture Dictionary
Spanish Picture Dictionary
My First Spanish and English
  Dictionary
Let's Learn Spanish Coloring Book
Let's Learn Spanish Coloring Book-
  Audiocassette Package
My World in Spanish Coloring Book
Let's Learn about Spain
Ya sé leer and Ya sé leer Workbook
Leamos un cuento
Spanish and Bilingual Readers
  Horas encantadas
  Había una vez
  Mother Goose on the Rio Grande
  ¡Hola amigos! Series
  Treasury of Children's Classics in
    Spanish and English
  Bilingual Fables
  Historietas en español
  Gabriel, the Happy Ghost
Soundsalive Spanish Phonics Review
  Cards
Sounds and Letters Audio-Visual
  Ronda del alfabeto
  A, E, I, O, U: Ahora cantas tú

"Cantando" We Learn (songbook and
  cassette)
La Navidad
Christmas in Spain
Christmas in Mexico
El alfabeto

**French**
Aventures 1, 2
Comment ça va? Learning Package
Comment ça va? Song Cassette
Quand tu seras grand Song Cassette
Le loup du Nord Song Cassette
Let's Learn French Picture Dictionary
French Picture Dictionary
Let's Learn French Coloring Book
Let's Learn French Coloring
  Book-Audiocassette Package
My World in French Coloring Book
Let's Learn about France
Je lis, tu lis
Exercices en français facile
Il était une fois
Bilingual Fables
Noël
Christmas in France
L'alphabet

**German**
Let's Learn German Picture Dictionary
German Picture Dictionary
Let's Learn German Coloring Book
Let's Learn German Coloring Book-
  Audiocassette Package
My World in German Coloring Book
Let's Learn about Germany
Es War Einmal
Weihnacht
Christmas in Germany

**Japanese**
Japanese for Children
Konnichi wa, Japan

**Italian**
Let's Learn Italian Picture Dictionary
Let's Learn Italian Coloring Book
Let's Learn Italian Coloring Book-
  Audiocassette Package
My World in Italian Coloring Book
Let's Learn about Italy
The Story Teller
Il Natale
Christmas in Italy

For further information or a current catalog, write:
National Textbook Company
a division of *NTC Publishing Group*
4255 West Touhy Avenue
Lincolnwood, Illinois 60646-1975 U.S.A.